Literacy

Language and Society Series

General editor
John Spencer
Director of the Institute of Modern English Language Studies,
University of Leeds

Loreto Todd *Pidgins and Creoles*
Michael Gregory and Susanne Carroll *Language and Situation*

Literacy
Writing, reading and social organisation

John Oxenham
Institute of Development Studies
University of Sussex

Routledge & Kegan Paul
London, Boston and Henley

First published in 1980
by Routledge & Kegan Paul Ltd
39 Store Street,
London WC1E 7DD,
9 Park Street,
Boston, Mass. 02108, USA and
Broadway House,
Newtown Road,
Henley-on-Thames,
Oxon RG9 1EN

Set in 10/11 Compugraphic Times English
and printed photolitho in Great Britain by
Ebenezer Baylis and Son Limited
The Trinity Press, Worcester, and London

British Library Cataloguing in Publication Data
Oxenham, John
    Literacy. – (Language and society series).
    1. Communications
    2. Books and reading
    I. Title   II. Series
301.2'1   P91   80–40367

ISBN 0 7100 0584 9
ISBN 0 7100 0619 5 Pbk

General editor's preface

We shall never know with any certainty how or when men first began to talk. The origins of human language lie deep in our prehistoric past, perhaps over a million years ago. All we can be sure of is that language made all mankind's subsequent social and economic evolution possible. Man's next major linguistic step, the invention of writing, occurred relatively recently however. The technique of writing is hardly more than 5,000 years old. We can therefore trace in detail the development of writing systems: from picture writing to ideogram and syllabary, and thence to the alphabet.

Writing, which provided a means of transferring messages from one place to another without the intervention of human voice or human memory, and of transmitting information in recorded form from one generation to another, gave a further powerful impetus to social, cultural and technological evolution. Not surprisingly, where the skills of reading and writing existed, they were much prized by elites, who were not normally inclined to extend them to the illiterate masses. Indeed, until the past century or so, the majority of the world's cultures had no writing system, and the bulk of the world's population lived and died without the benefit of literacy.

Those who read this page may well take their capacity to do so for granted. This is perhaps unwise. For it is only during the last three or four generations that literacy has been at all widespread. Only in the past century and a half have writing systems been devised for many of the world's languages. Only since the introduction of compulsory schooling for children has literacy spread to a majority of the populations of even the most developed societies in the world. And in many societies, even today, the majority of people are illiterate. Almost a billion of the world's total population cannot read or write.

It is not easy to specify with any precision the role played by literacy in societies past and present, or the functions of literacy in the life of the individual. Both vary from culture to culture, and from age to age. Certainly, the introduction of writing into a society has always produced change. And the invention of printing clearly hastened shifts towards increasingly literate cultures. It is difficult to conceive of advanced technology without literacy and numeracy; equally, it is hard to imagine large-scale organisations, whether commercial or bureaucratic, being able to function without the use of writing. And today it is argued that literacy is a universal human right.

Yet it is still not clear under what circumstances literacy can best be extended and maintained. Nor is it clear how, once literacy is established, it can most fruitfully be sustained. In the present century technology has made it possible for spoken language to be sent instantaneously from one end of the earth to the other, and for speech to be stored and retransmitted at will. What are the uses of literacy now? Literacy raises complex questions, deserving the attention of everyone interested in education, social evolution, or economic development. There are linguistic, psychological, cultural, economic and political dimensions to be taken into account; and historical perspectives are also necessary, if we are to gain a comprehensive understanding of literacy and its relationship to human progress. This volume succeeds remarkably in doing this, within a relatively small compass.

Its author, John Oxenham, is an outstanding specialist on literacy, for his is an authority based both on scholarly learning and on long practical field experience. At the Institute of Development Studies at the University of Sussex he pursues research into the relation between literacy, schooling and human productivity. He is widely consulted on literacy and community development programmes. In the early 1960s he was charged with the development of an adult literacy campaign in seven languages in Zambia. Seven years later the campaign was awarded the Nadya Krupskaya prize for the best-organised literacy programme in the world. He subsequently worked on a rural education project in Indonesia under UNESCO auspices; and has planned curricula in Turkey for a campaign to combine literacy with training in agriculture, home economics, nutrition and family planning.

Sociolinguistics is a large and expanding field of interdisciplinary activity, focusing attention in a variety of ways on the interaction of linguistic and social phenomena. For students in a broad range of humane disciplines it can offer new and stimulating perspectives. It is the purpose of this series to offer brief, readable and scholarly introductions to the main themes and topics covered by current sociolinguistic studies.

John Spencer

Contents

Introductory note

Only a decade ago, in 1968, Jack Goody edited a collection of studies of literacy. In his introduction he remarked on a surprising fact. Although writing, and hence reading, have been practised in many civilisations for some 5,000 years, how they might affect the societies which invented or adopted them is a question which has been little explored. Their possible effects on the individual have been looked at more, but not for very long. John Guthrie in 1976 briefly traced the history of enquiries into how reading is actually learned. Up to the end of the nineteenth century, there had apparently been only thirty studies published in English. By 1970 that number had mushroomed to more than four thousand and its rate of growth has been accelerating since.

The study of literacy is clearly part of the modern proliferation of sciences. Equally, it is a young branch of investigation. Its growing pains are compounded by another fact of modern science, for which the ruling code-word is 'interdisciplinarity'. Literacy as a phenomenon requires for its explanation the attention of at least eight academic disciplines. They range from studies concerned with the microelectrical impulses of the human brain to those which examine the struggles between the governing few and the subordinated masses of great empires. Physiology, psychology, sociology, economics, the development of technology, political science, history, archaeology all have indispensable contributions to make to the complete understanding of the invention, uses and repercussions of literacy. It is another case of the now familiar dialectic between specialisation and synthesis.

It is still too early for a definitive synthesis. This book is no more than an introductory exploration of the roles of literacy in the lives of individuals and their societies. For those who decide to embark on more comprehensive syntheses of their own, lists of helpful books accompany each chapter. They are an acknowledgment of the opportunities and independence which the individual can gain from literacy.

Chapter one
Illiteracy today

Helping others to achieve literacy has been a concern of some people not for decades, nor even for centuries, but for millennia. Their effectiveness has waxed and waned at different times in different societies. The high point of their success is the present century. Writing and reading were invented five thousand years ago. Only now are they proclaimed as part of the inalienable rights of man and only now is universal literacy on national and international agendas. Indeed, literacy had to wait until the nineteenth century A.D. before it was even collected as an item of social statistics; and until the twentieth century before a government – the communists of Russia – embarked on a specific crusade to spread it swiftly among the entire population, school-age and adult. The crescendo of the drive for literacy is reflected in three facts: first, in the mid-nineteenth century, less than one in ten of the world's adult population could read and write; second, by the third quarter of the twentieth century, the proportion which had gained literacy was very nearly seven in ten; third, this progress occurred not with a static population, but, as has been urgently bruited, with a population that has itself been expanding at an exponential rate – from $1 \cdot 2$ billion in 1850 to $2 \cdot 4$ billion in 1950 to almost 4 billion in 1975. Clearly the 'struggle against illiteracy', as it is often termed, has been fairly successful. Though still incomplete by a considerable margin, it has more than coped both with the desire that more and more people should be literate and with the problem that the number of people to learn literacy has been growing all the time.

What I want to explore in the rest of this book is why there should have been such a prodigious effort to spread literacy, and whether the reasons were sound. Before doing so, I want to set out the situation on literacy, as it was estimated in 1970, and to remark some of its characteristics. For the moment, I shall use the terms 'literate' and 'illiterate' imprecisely, because giving them a definition that is at once universally valid and easily grasped has long been a bane of educational statisticians. 'Literate' here means 'able to read and write', and 'illiterate' means 'not so able'. Whether 'able to read' might include the comprehension of learned treatises or just the gist of a poster advertising a jumble sale is a point we shall neglect for the time being, together with the issue whether 'able to write' implies merely the ability to sign one's own name or expressive skills somewhat more developed than that.

In 1971, some 780 million people over the age of fifteen all over the world were classed as illiterate. Their number will probably increase slightly every year, so that by 1980 they will total perhaps 820 million. This calculation assumes a growth rate of one-half of one per cent annually. For the sake of comparison, the growth rate of whole populations of the world will be slightly under two per cent annually. That is, the numbers of illiterates will be growing more slowly than the rest of the population, which means of course that the proportion of illiterates will continue to decline steadily. Such a cheerful assertion will hold only if the assumptions behind it hold. As will be noted later, there have been times when societies have actually lost their literacy.

Whatever proportion they form of the total population of the world, 800 million are a lot of people. Even if they were distributed evenly over the face of the earth, they would constitute a noticeable minority group. What makes them more noticeable is that they tend to be concentrated in certain regions. The United Nations Educational, Scientific and Cultural Organisation (UNESCO), pointed out in 1965 that the world map of illiteracy coincided very closely with the world map of poverty. The poorer countries of the world tend to have the highest proportions of illiterates, though there are a few exceptions. Africa, taken as a whole, is almost three-quarters illiterate, and so is half of Asia. The twenty-five poorest countries show rates of illiteracy in excess of 80 per cent. The rich countries of America and Europe, on the other hand, have achieved almost universal literacy – although, indeed, even that statement will have to be modified.

The unevenness in global distribution has its counterpart within the regions and within countries also. In Asia, rates of adult illiteracy range from 12 per cent in South Korea to 77 per cent in Bangladesh; among the Arab states from 14 per cent in the Lebanon to 90 per cent in the Yemen; in Africa from 20 per cent in Mauritius to 95 per cent in Somalia; in Latin America from 10 per cent in Chile to 62 per cent in Guatemala.

For the situation inside countries, South Korea provides an illustration. Her overall rate of illiteracy, 12 per cent, is very low, but even so, it masks some wide discrepancies. Only 5 per cent of the males are illiterate: for practical purposes, South Korea could claim universal literacy for the men. The corollary of that, though, is that nearly four times as many women as men are illiterate! The gap between the men and the women is substantial. We shall return to it in a moment.

Between the men themselves, two further general gaps appear. Among the urban men, only two of every hundred are classed as illiterate. Four times as many of their rural compatriots carry the label. A similar contrast exists between the men of the upper income groups and those of the lower.

South Korea provides a neat paradigm of the rest of the world, even though it is in many respects an advanced country. The gap between the men and the women is echoed in nearly all developing countries. Particularly marked examples occur in Africa and among the Arab states. To extend this observation: the higher the overall rate of illiteracy for a country, the wider will be the absolute gap between men and women. Of course, where illiteracy is nearly universal, there will be small differences between the sexes. Even so, the few who would be literate in such circumstances will be overwhelmingly male. The men learn literacy first; their womenfolk are kept or linger some way behind them. The fact may simply be noted here. It will recur when we consider the economic and political uses of literacy. As would be expected, the differences among the women are as great as those among the men. Although slightly worse off even than the rural men, the urban women of South Korea class only 9 per cent of themselves as illiterate. By contrast, fully three times that proportion of their rural sisters are similarly described. The male:female, urban:rural disparities are most starkly captured by setting the South Korean urban males alongside the rural females: 2 per cent of the former and 27 per cent of the latter – thirteen times the proportion – are illiterate.

Similarly echoed is the gap between the rural and urban populations: the higher the country's rate of illiteracy, the greater will be the disparity between the villages and the towns. The towns learn literacy first. This fact, too, is connected with the roles of literacy in a society. So also is the fact that the richer groups of a community tend to make more rapid and more thorough use of the institutions through which literacy is acquired. For one reason or another, the poorer groups cannot avail themselves fully either of schools for their children or of compensatory programmes for themselves. In passing we may note that the richer groups tend to include the rulers and more influential sections of a society.

The pattern of inequalities in literacy is of course not a new phenomenon. It was noted within Europe in the mid-nineteenth century. Whereas Sweden and Scotland were respectively 90 and 80 per cent literate, Spain and Italy could boast only 25 per cent. And in Italy in 1871, while only 42 per cent of the people of Piedmont were illiterate, 68 of the Tuscans were, and so were 88 per cent of the people in the southern region of Basilicata. Further, in all the regions of Italy the men showed higher rates of literacy than the women. On the whole, too, the contrasts held between town and village and between income groups (Cipolla, 1969). Such exceptions as there were – Scotland, Sweden and Switzerland were all more literate than England, yet poorer, less industrialised and less urbanised – can be plausibly explained by the uses made of literacy within the society.

I have hinted several times at the roles and uses of literacy within societies; I have indicated that in the past 100 years there has been a drive towards universal literacy; and I have at least implied that, where illiteracy now exists, it is considered a problem and, *a fortiori*, that, where it looms large, it is officially felt to be a grave disadvantage. Evidence for the last statement is to be found abundantly in the publications of UNESCO and in the development plans of perhaps a hundred countries. It is also to be seen in the numerous literacy campaigns mounted by governments and private organisations, and perhaps at its clearest in the resources expended by the United Nations Development Programme (UNDP), UNESCO and a dozen or so governments – Algeria, Ecuador, Iran, Tanzania among them – on the Experimental World Literacy Programme. Why should this be so? In the next chapter, the various reasons why illiteracy has been transformed, so to speak, from the normal and unexceptionable state of most human beings to one of the scourges of human society, will be explored.

Further reading

Leon Bataille, ed. (1976), *A Turning Point for Literacy,* London, Pergamon Press. Chapter 1 (Working Document 1) – 'Literacy in the World since 1969' is a survey by the UNESCO Secretariat of progress and trends in the eradication of illiteracy around the world.

Carlo Cipolla (1969), *Literacy And Development In The West*, Harmondsworth, Pelican Books.

Chapter two
The demand for literacy

A qualification needs to be made about the present-day concern for universal literacy: it is not equally distributed. It is perhaps least felt – if it is felt at all – in communities and societies where literacy is entirely superfluous to ordinary life. The small mountain tribes of New Guinea or villagers living in the inaccessible regions of a number of African states make no use of literacy in their routines of hunting, subsistence agriculture, house-keeping, litigation, story-telling or dancing. Nor, if offered the bald opportunity to read and write, would they necessarily jump at it eagerly. Like the Fijians in the nineteenth century and others, they might need to suspect that the mysterious symbols possessed magic powers or some other desirable value, before they made any effort to master them (Clammer, 1975). While these certainly are extreme examples, marginal to our purpose, they help explain why so many of the campaigns to make small communities and even whole nations literate have been so ill-rewarded. It seems to be true that illiterate people with little contact with the doings of literate societies experience small need or desire for literacy. Indeed, it may be the case that the greater the degree of illiteracy in a society, the less will be the concern of the illiterates about being illiterate. Conversely, the greater the degree of literacy, the greater will be the anxiety of the illiterate either to acquire literacy or to disguise his illiteracy and operate as though literate.

These observations imply an essential point about the skills of reading and writing: they are means to various ends. If the ends are not perceived or, being perceived, are not of much importance to the perceiver, then there is neither ground nor motivation to acquire the means to them. It would follow then that any pressure to promote literacy would usually accompany some larger purpose: literacy would be *for* something.

A second point implied by these observations is that the presence and utilisation of literacy depend on the nature of the society in question. It is patently possible for societies of hunters, gatherers, subsistence cultivators, nomadic cattle-herders, and even, as in the cases of the Kikuyu of Kenya and the market mammies of West Africa, for traders to get along to their own large satisfaction without being able to read and write at all. It is also possible, as in the case of Europe up until the seventeenth and eighteenth centuries and, say India or Indonesia even now, for urban and commercial societies to function with an illiterate majority, and a tiny class of literates to man the apparatuses of state, religion, commerce and industry.

This second illustration returns us to the unevenness of concerns for universal literacy. In largely illiterate nations, where rulers are in no pressing hurry to share power – or, put differently, to introduce the chaos and inefficiencies of some form of democracy, in so far as literacy is perceived as a wedge for democracy – its spread will either be discouraged or at least not helped. To say this is, of course, to indicate again the instrumental nature of literacy.

Besides being bound up with purposes, however, literacy is nearly always associated with some notion of education, enlightenment and mental expansion. To point this out is to remind ourselves that the most important vehicle of literacy is the school. Campaigns to make adults literate tend to be given more publicity than the humdrum routines of the school – though the content and direction of these routines are currently and nearly everywhere at the centre of public debate – but it is the school which is allocated even more than a lion's share of resources of money, materials and personnel. A random review of the educational expenditures of almost any government – perhaps especially those with high rates of illiteracy – will show that schools and universities account in most cases for more than 95 per cent of the allocations. Consequently, when we talk of the push for literacy, we mean in bulk the spread of schooling, which of course involves more than merely learning to read and write. If we hark back to the fact that the majority, 70 per cent, of the world's population is now literate, we are acknowledging the prodigious efforts and resources which have been devoted all over the world – but with varying intensity and sincerity – to getting children into school. Again, a random review of educational budgets since about 1950 will illustrate concretely just how heavily education weighs in the policies of governments. By 1975, indeed, some countries were pouring as much as a third of their annual budgets into their schools and universities. I mention these facts simply to stress that literacy has generally been part of wider programmes of education and has not been a self-sufficient goal on its own; and hence to repeat both that literacy is always *for* something and that it is related to the way a society directs its functioning. At the same time, I must be careful not to understate the importance of literacy: it remains a foundation stone of most current education.

We may now take up the question posed at the end of the last chapter: what explains the present general concern for literacy (and education)? In the light of the preceding paragraphs the query may be rephrased: what purpose or set of purposes has brought literacy into such prominent focus? As with all human affairs, the answer is composed of not one, but of several coinciding factors. Over the past four centuries a variety of needs and pressures have been gathering force to require that most people in most of today's societies should be schooled and literate to at least some degree. Some of the pressures spring from each other and are mutually reinforcing, but it will be useful to review them one by one.

Writing in its fullest sense – as word and sound symbols and not simply as picture-signs – was invented some 5,000 years ago. The oldest examples available to us are ledger tablets in Old Sumerian. Writing seems to have had its roots in commerce, in the records of transactions. Interesting support for this notion comes from the Chinese legend that the inventor of writing was Fu Hsi, who coincidentally was the founder of commerce. My purpose in mentioning this is to call attention to the development of commerce between

Europe and the rest of the world during the fifteenth and subsequent centuries. The merchant traders, their clerks, their
accountants, and the captains of their ships, would all have
found some degree of literacy extremely convenient, if not
nigh indispensable, in their dealings. Enjoying the use of
literacy themselves, they would have found irksome its lack in
their colleagues and subordinates with similar functions and,
in the nature of organisation men, would seek as co-workers
men with skills like their own. In this way, the needs and
purposes of commerce would have contributed to the demand
for literate people and, in the concomitant willingness to pay
a bit more for the literate over the unlettered man, would
have encouraged people to learn literacy.

Sea captains, besides being accountable for cargoes, also
needed to read maps and charts and to keep pace with the
developing arts of navigation. They were part of the
beginnings of the technological revolution which brought
printing, gunpowder and firearms, strides in merchant and
warship building, and which would gather increasing
momentum through the industrial revolution to the present
day. Each step created needs for craftsmen and managers
who could at least read and interpret plans and instructions.
As the wealth of societies increased, so too did the demand
for such craftsmen and so correspondingly did the numbers
of those who wished to learn to read and write. Eventually,
the nature of the industrial revolution helped to make it clear
that schooling and literacy were necessary for virtually the
entire population, and thus smooth the way for compulsory
education.

Additionally, of course, the invention of printing in the
fifteenth century eventually made it more worthwhile to learn
to read, for reading matter was becoming more widely available. The flood of print was nowhere near the proportions it
reached when mechanically powered presses were developed
in the nineteenth century. Nevertheless, the gradual seeping
of books, pamphlets and perhaps especially the Christian
Bible out from the richer or otherwise more privileged groups
like the clergy, coupled with the mystique and prestige already

arrogated to book learning by these same privileged people, would have helped reinforce the demand for literature and literacy.

In company with the growth of wealth and technology in Europe, there was waxing also the apparatus of the state. The emergence of the nation-states and colonial empires from the sixteenth century on, with increasingly strong centres of government, necessitated systems of administration and communication which could not practicably be supported without literacy. The application of laws and regulations, the levying and accounting of taxes, the multiplying petty business of central and subordinate governments led in turn to the multiplication of employments requiring literacy.

All this was occurring on the secular side of life. But religion, too, was contributing a pressure. The rise and success of Protestant Christianity in Northern Europe gave an impetus to the reading of the Bible. Men were to read God's word for themselves and to interpret it according to their own consciences, with guidance from more qualified pastors. The authority of the clergy of what was seen as a corrupt and ungodly organisation, the Church of Rome, was rejected as the sole interpreter of the Gospel. Accordingly, it is not surprising that the Protestant countries of Sweden, Scotland and Switzerland should have displayed even as early as the seventeenth century rather higher rates of literacy than the Catholic South in Italy: 35–45 per cent against 20–30 per cent. It might even be hazarded that the motivation provided by religion in Scotland helped outweigh the forces of commerce and technology in England, for it will be recalled from the previous chapter that *circa* 1850 Scotland's rate of literacy was higher than England's.

Independence of reading and judgment in religion was not unrelated to the growth of independence of judgment in politics and hence to the development of forms of democracy in North America and in Europe. Political debate, tracts, pamphlets would have contributed to a climate stimulating to the acquisition of literacy. The gradual loosening of the right to vote from restriction to people of property to the inclusion of people who were literate was yet a further incentive for schooling and education. In this area a certain conflict of interest can be discerned. Commerce, technology and administration might all be generating vaster demands for educated, literate personnel, yet the ruling classes who shared in all three engines of demand, not yet convinced of the practicability of democracy – the French Revolution had been no encouragement – were nervous of the effects of schooling on the masses.

About ten years before the Revolution, the French Attorney General had written:

> Never before have there been so many students . . . even
> the working people want to study . . . the Brothers of
> Christian Doctrine, called the *Ignorantins*, are pursuing
> a fatal policy; they are teaching people to read and write
> who should have learnt only to draw and to handle
> planes and files but who now no longer wish to do so.
> The good of society demands that the knowledge of the
> people should not exceed what is necessary in their
> occupation. Every man who sees further than his dull
> daily round will never follow it out bravely and
> patiently. Among the common people it is really only
> necessary for those to learn reading and writing who live
> by means of these accomplishments, or who need them
> in their daily tasks. (Cipolla, 1969)

Such hesitations were overruled in time. Yet it is piquant to note not only that there were literacy tests for voting rights in the southern United States until quite recently, but also that in the early 1960s, in the countries of the defunct Central African Federation (now separately Malawi, Zimbabwe-Rhodesia and Zambia), grades of education were combined with levels of property and income to award voting rights. The assumption implicit here – not shared by a country like India with 75 per cent of her population still illiterate – is that literacy and a tincture of education are necessary to a person who is to take a rational part in the politics of his society. Its most forthright expression was perhaps given by Lenin when he helped launch the great campaign to make Russia literate: 'an illiterate man is non-political; first he must be taught how to read.' There is in this a clear belief that the skills of literacy have much to do with transforming a person – to use the phraseology of current fashion – from a passive object of history to an autonomous subject aware of the nature of his society and able to assist in changing it. To what extent such a belief is tenable will be considered later.

Less powerfully perhaps than the forces of commerce or politics, but no less real, the appetites whetted by cultural literature and the newspapers must also have contributed to the demand for literacy. The technological improvements which drove down the prices of books and newspapers, while simultaneously enabling vast numbers of them to be published – the paperback revolution of the 1930s was only the latest step – help explain the rising consumption of literature of various types and the corresponding use of literacy. Supplementing the supply and helping to fuel the demand was, of course, the spread of public libraries. Tables 2.1, 2.2 and 2.3 afford some idea of these processes.

Table 2.1 Book production in the world (number of titles published)

	1955	1965	1976	1955 %	1965 %	1976 %
World	269000	426000	591000	100	158	219
Africa	3000	7000	11000	100	233	366
America, North	14000	58000	91000	100	414	650
America, Latin	11000	19000	31000	100	172	281
Asia	54000	61000	100000	100	113	185
Europe	131000	200000	269000	100	152	205
Oceania	1000	5000	5000	100	500	500
USSR	55000	76000	84000	100	138	152

Table 2.2 Percentage distribution of population and book production in the world

	Population	Book Production
World	100·0	100·0
Africa	13·0	1·9
America, North	7·5	15·4
America, Latin	10·5	5·2
Asia	45·2	16·9
Europe	15·0	45·6
Oceania	0·7	0·8
USSR	8·1	14·2

Table 2.3 Sample of published works loaned out by Public Libraries (mainly in 1974)

	Works loaned	Population	Loans per capita
Denmark	83·6 million	c.5 million	16·7
Germany, West	130·0 million	c.61 million	2·1
Italy	9·9 million	c.56 million	0·17
Sweden	71·1 million	c.8 million	8·8
UK*	600·0 million	c.56 million	10·7
USA	892·8 million	c.215 million	4·1

Sources: UNESCO, *Statistical Yearbook*, 1977, Tables 11.1–3, 10.6.
       *Hugh Jenkins, *The Culture Gap*, 1979, London, Marion Boyars.

In sum, the combined pressures of commerce, technology, government, politics, religion and culture have created needs, rewards and demands for literacy. This has been true most obviously in the industrialised states of Europe, North America and Japan. It is particularly true of their industrial centres, the cities, and of their industrial workforces. Except where Protestant Christianity and a democratic political ethic have been strong, the rural areas, the agricultural workforces, the women, and especially rural housewives, have tended to lag. If the acquisition of the tools of literacy is indeed a response to a need or to an incentive, it is easy to see why these groups should not have been as swift as the others in making themselves literate. It is also easy to see why the agrarian states of the world or those with regimes dominated by small groups unwilling to share power or those subordinated to the interests of an imperial industrialised centre, should have lagged in terms of international comparisons.

However, since about 1920 and with even greater thrust since 1945, governments and international agencies have been deliberately pushing towards universal literacy, mainly through the school, but also with less effectiveness and perhaps less determination, through special programmes and campaigns for adults. The demand for literacy is being led less by felt needs on the part of the illiterate or on the part of employers, or by voluntary agencies with special interests, and much more by official action backed by resources from the state. Up until the middle of the twentieth century, governments – apart from one or two outstanding exceptions like the communist regime of Russia or Atatürk's regime in Turkey – had at most played a minor supportive role in adult literacy. Between 1950 and 1970 by contrast, very nearly 100 governments had launched official national literacy campaigns.

Why this should be so is perhaps most easily explained by the 'yeast' effect, which literacy is thought to operate. Support for this belief has come from various sources. From sociologists came studies which suggested that some kind of 'modernisation syndrome' was associated with literacy. Surveying a number of Middle Eastern countries, Daniel Lerner identified the capacity for 'empathy'; the capacity to put oneself into the shoes of another, as a significant indicator of flexibility, adaptability, broadness of interests, willingness to accept change, readiness to initiate change, to innovate. All this appeared related to a certain critical level of literacy within a person and within a society (Lerner, 1958). Taking the theme further and looking at countries in Asia, Latin America and Africa, Alex Inkeles and his associates found schooling and literacy to be linked to certain aspects of 'modern man' (Inkeles and Holsinger, 1974). Everett Rogers and his colleagues seemed overall to support the notion that proneness to adopt innovations was related to the level of literacy and education (Rogers and Shoemaker, 1971). Economists threw in their weight by pointing to certain correlations. Although the first country to industrialise, England, had lower levels of literacy than much of Europe at the period of early industrialisation, nevertheless it was the more literate countries which most speedily imported the industrial revolution. Further, countries with less than a certain level of literacy and schooling appeared to experience great difficulty in modernising and otherwise developing themselves. For instance, C. Arnold Anderson began a well-known essay on 'Literacy and Schooling on the Development Threshold: Some Historical Cases' with these words: 'Very broadly, the data appears to support a generalisation reached also by cross-sectional analysis of contemporary societies: about 40 per cent of adult literacy or of primary enrollment is a threshold for economic development' (Anderson and Bowman, 1966). Also, it was an obvious fact that the countries with the highest rates of literacy and schooling were also those with high incomes and high capacities for technological development. In addition, calculations were elaborated to contend that the advance of a society depended not merely on its capital, its natural resources, its technology but also on the education (and hence literacy) of its workers. Educated people tended to be more productive, if only because they could handle more sophisticated machinery more competently.

This view was underpinned by the experiences of industrial employers who found schooled and literate people not only easier to train but also apparently more able to hold on to what they learned. The copper-mining companies of Zambia, for instance, had the impression that an illiterate who had been trained by them lost much of his skill if he returned to his home village for long leave; whereas personnel with schooling and literacy seemed not to suffer such problems. Such experience was echoed by trainers working in agricultural extension: literate farmers seemed to be faster and more effective learners, and they were able to take and utilise new information much more rapidly than their illiterate fellows. Besides, it was found that illiterate people from illiterate societies have little ability to grasp or to create abstract concepts; they seem by and large to operate less from general principles and more from concrete, limited instances. Brilliant exceptions could, of course, always be cited, but the average illiterate thus appeared to have a relatively restricted capacity for absorbing training. Napoleon is said to have had great trouble in getting peasants and illiterates to march and drill. His exasperation drove him to tying their feet with 50cm. lengths of rope in the hope of inducing the necessary sense of precision, uniformity and repeatability.

Whilst these studies and less systematic experiences were being published and assessed, most governments – perhaps especially those newly liberated from colonial masters – had already decided that their societies and economies must be made richer and better. Their populations were already accelerating into the so-called crisis of expectations. Education and literacy were already perceived as important both to the transformation sought officially and to the better living desired privately. The findings of the social scientists served to justify and to reinforce policies already launched. Education and literacy (through school mainly) were promoted on the grounds that not only were they the rights of every human being called on to function in modern society, but, even more, they were areas for rational and generous investment by the state. In effect, literacy and schooling were not simply tools to be given to illiterates to meet their needs, they were in addition transformers, enabling the illiterates to perceive old phenomena, long tolerated as inevitable features of life, as problems requiring new solutions, and to make fuller use of resources and services and take the initiative in changing their lives. Put slightly differently, literacy and schooling were seen as technologies, which by their very use were to transform their users. Moreover, they were regarded as technologies indispensable to rapid socio-economic development. A particularly eloquent quotation from Iraq will serve to illustrate the point:

> The high rate of illiteracy among citizens, particularly in rural areas, is considered to be the most serious and dangerous constraint impeding the political, economic and social progression of the country. With the present high rate of illiteracy, it is impossible to raise the standard of the masses, build up an advanced revolutionary society capable of confronting the problems of the age and its complicated requisites. It is also not possible for our country to contribute to the building up of a united socialist Arab nation. Therefore, the fight against illiteracy within the shortest possible time is considered the most important sphere of our struggle and activities.
> (Iraq Government, Act 142, 1974)

While these general attitudes to literacy and school existed, they did not of course answer the more detailed questions relating to the allocation of resources. Given that the means to school everyone to an adequate standard of literacy immediately were not available, and given that basic literacy would not be sufficient for managers, or doctors, engineers, or teachers, what were to be the priorities, for priorities there simply had to be? The outcomes of the trading over priorities between public interests and private demands have largely been that the higher levels of schooling (and universities) have captured disproportionate shares of the resources to hand; and the areas where the need for literacy has not been acute or the demand for literacy not vocally effective have tended to remain illiterate, either through being denied access to schools and special programmes, or through substantial rates of dropout from them. Hence it is that the poor, the rural, the politically less active and the women remain prominent in the statistics of illiteracy.

Further reading

C. Arnold Anderson and Mary Jean Bowman, eds (1966), *Education and Economic Development*, London, Frank Cass.

Mary Jean Bowman and C. Arnold Anderson (1963), 'Concerning The Role Of Education In Development', pp. 247–79 in Clifford Geertz, *Old Societies and New States*, New York, Free Press.

Chapter three
Literacy and the individual

That literacy should be seized as a tool by those who need it or can use it to gain rewards is natural. That it should be regarded as a very special kind of technology, able radically to transform its user and his society, requires investigation. The idea of the magic, at times the sacredness and power, of literacy is perhaps as old as the technology itself. In several societies, the ability to read and write has been preserved as the prerogative of either a priestly caste or a small ruling group. It is true that mystiques of one degree or another have grown up round hunting, blacksmithing and nearly every ancient craft. Trades had their guilds and their secrets. Nevertheless, none of them has commanded quite the same aura of almost preternatural power as literacy, nor has any of them enjoyed status as one of the marks of civilised man: up until very recently in history literacy has generally been the perquisite of small and usually very influential groups in a society. Why should this be so? In this chapter we shall examine in more detail what we mean by literacy and what it entails. Thereafter, the implications it might have for an individual and for a society will be explored.

In essence, literacy is simply a means of embodying language in a visual form. (For blind people, literacy is tactile but that is a special case.) Speech is a mode using the mouth and the ear (oral/aural) to communicate experiences, information, ideas and argument between people. It is a code and convention, in which certain sounds and combinations of sounds are created and accepted as conveying certain limited ranges of meaning. In very few instances are such codes perfect in communication: ambiguities and misunderstandings occur, sometimes by design! But that is not to our purpose here. Since literacy is derived from spoken language,

19

it is in effect a code of a code, the visual form of an oral/aural medium.

However, literacy supports not merely the function of communication. It embraces, too, the functions of recording and storing, the functions of memory. Indeed, it may well have begun as an aid to memory and later developed into a medium of communication. In its capacity, literacy goes beyond speech and memory. Whereas the first is fleeting, impermanent and hard to recapture and the second unreliable, inconstant and, despite the occasional prodigy, severely limited in the amount it can store, increasingly limited with increasing age! and suspiciously selective – the code of literacy is as constant and as permanent as the materials in which it is embodied. Again, where only memory and speech are available, one person cannot use the information held by another, unless that other is physically present. Literacy by contrast permits a person access to information independently of others.

The need for such a versatile medium of record, storage and communication seems to have been felt wherever human society developed beyond rudimentary forms of subsistence, organisation and transaction. Several devices were invented by different societies to meet the need. Symbols of some sort were necessary. Pictures and picture signs were an obvious avenue and formed the early attempts. But other kinds of symbols could be, and indeed were, used. While the hieroglyphs of the ancient Egyptians are perhaps the best-known form of early writing, the Incas of Peru developed their system of *Quipu* with strings and knots of various lengths, shapes and colours, the Indians of North America elaborated their *Wampums*, with belts of shells and beads, the Yoruba of West Africa worked out their way with the shells of the cowrie mussel. Using *letters*, whether on clay, stone, papyrus or paper, was but an outcome of long series of efforts to improve the recording, storage and communication of all the content of language. Letter symbols differ from pictorial and other types only – but crucially – in the quantity and subtlety of the communications they can bear.

Figure 3.1 Stages of writing simplified

	Approximate period of appearance
Pictures	pre-historic
Stylised signs (agreed by convention)	pre-3000 B.C.
Pictographic and Logographic (signs for whole words)	*c.* 3100 B.C.
Phonetic (writing based on sounds)	
– syllabic (signs for combinations of sounds which are only parts of words)	*c.* 1700 B.C.
– alphabetic (signs for the single separate sounds which make up words)	*c.* 1200 B.C.

This difference is so easily remarked in passing, that its full import might be missed. Symbols or codes like, for example, road signs, pictures illustrating how to operate a machine, or even hieroglyphs can convey single thoughts or even sequences of ideas, events, instructions. They can impart the sense of all these without being bound to a particular form of words. That 'A picture is worth a thousand words' is often true and different verbal descriptions of a picture may well mobilise many different words in many different sequences. But it is also often true that a thousand words can tell a great deal more than a single picture. And a thousand written words can convey much more information with much more economy of ingenuity, effort, art and space than a series of pictures. Equally important, whereas drawing good pictures demands skills which are fairly exceptional, writing with acceptable legibility is a skill attainable by most people. *Quipu* string and *Wampum* belts can undeniably record and impart a variety and complexity of messages. Even so, they inherently cannot match the variety and complexity of language to the same degree that letters can; there are obvious limits to the shapes and volumes they can assume. Through the invention of letters man gave himself a medium of communication almost as easy as, and certainly more powerful than, speech itself. For, while 800 million adults may indeed be illiterate and while millions more may fail to learn to attain literacy in ten years of schooling, it remains true that millions more of children of six years upwards do learn to read and write with fair rapidity.

The first applications of letters seem to have been as notes of transactions in the cities of Mesopotamia about 5,000 years ago. They were simple aids to memory, to keep track of trading, accounts and debts. They might have been merely private symbols or codes for the writers, solely for their own use and for no public purpose. In that case, they would have been like the idiosyncratic shorthands which students, secretaries and others who need to record much invent for themselves. And they would probably be unintelligible today. However, because they were not private codes, but public ones in wide use, it has been possible to decipher or to decode them. Two points are implied in this observation.

First, some people must have been busy inventing, elaborating and improving the codes of record and communication. They were the encoders and their successors are still with us today. A notable and dramatic example was Kemal Atatürk who in 1928 decided that Turkish must no longer be coded in the Arabic script. Although he opted for the Latin script instead, he and his colleagues found that that, too, was not entirely suited to the Turkish language and consequently modified it with both omissions and additions into an alphabet of twenty-nine letters with eight vowels. Closer to home, George Bernard Shaw left a large sum of money for the re-coding of the English language along what he considered more rational lines, but his executors have had to give up the case as hopeless. Similarly, a number of Chinese scholars and officials, having worked for many years on the modification of the enormous volume of the Chinese code,

Figure 3.2 Simplified diagrammatic history of major scripts

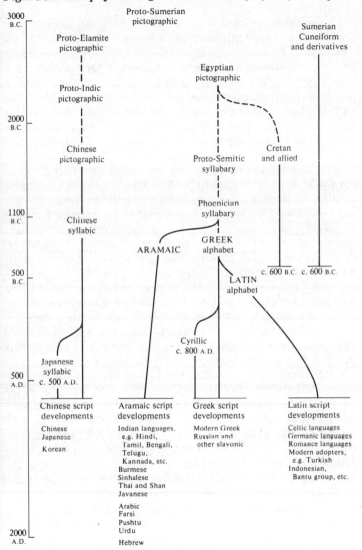

were rewarded only in 1979 by a decision to change gradually to a phonetic script.

These three examples of code-creators underscore the second point about public codes: they have to be accepted by their public before they can be effective. That is, there needs to be a convention or widespread, even if tacit, acceptance that a given code will be accorded a common use and a common interpretation. Atatürk had the political power to change Turkey's code almost overnight and to have it accepted by the nation; Shaw patently had no such power, despite the money he provided; the Chinese reformers, whatever the power of the central government, did not feel they had sufficient acceptance among the people generally to press for the kind of action taken by Atatürk. There has then to be a body of decoders, whom the code-creators must always keep in view. This point draws attention to the social nature of literacy; because it involves communication, the communicator needs, if he wants to be understood, to adjust himself to the capacities and even whims of the receiver. Literacy is in part a social transaction. How deeply a particular codification can be enmeshed with social emotions like national pride and prejudice, and hence with politics, is already hinted by the three examples. It will be discussed again in due course.

A word on my use of the terms 'encoder' and 'decoder'. For most literate people, reading is a good deal easier than writing. It is simpler and less taxing to decode what someone has put together – provided the key to the code is already known and the encoder does not vary the code through wildly inconsistent spelling! – than to put together something oneself. This is reflected in the widespread observations that people on the whole learn to read faster than they learn to write, that many people, particularly where illiteracy is high, can read but cannot write, and that even in almost completely literate societies reading is practised a good deal more than writing. A moment's thought shows why this should be so. Reading requires eyesight, a knowledge of the code in use, a knowledge of the language encoded and the learned ability to decode rapidly enough both to abstract the meaning of the individual words and to synthesise them into a coherent whole. Writing by contrast requires not only all this, but also the ability to formulate and to marshal thoughts in some satisfactory order, to spell them out letter by letter, and then to transmit them through some relatively fine movements co-ordinating mind, eye and fingers, into the code in a manner sufficiently clear to be decipherable by an intending decoder. Because writing requires such a combination and co-ordination of effort, most people are tired more rapidly by writing than they are by reading.

My reason for raising this point is to try to gain some appreciation for those original code-creators, who in many civilisations developed the first visual codes for language. For English we have a code which is phonemic. The letters of our alphabet are attached to sounds which by themselves are meaningless and each letter signifies a very limited range of sounds. English is imperfectly phonemic precisely because it does admit a range of interpretation for many of its letters. The letter *a*, for example, can indicate at least six sounds, as the following sentence demonstrates:

'A car smashed the mare at the gate as she ate!'
 1 2   3   4   3   5   3   6

A perfectly phonemic alphabet would have only one letter per distinctive sound. It would thereby avoid uncertainties on spelling or encoding and on re-sounding or decoding. This is what Atatürk tried to achieve with his reform of Turkish writing, what the Finnish alphabet seems to have achieved and what the proponents of the Pitman Initial Teaching Alphabet for English want, too.

Attaching letters to sounds may appear a relatively simple operation. However, the fact that English, with its very highly developed literature, remains imperfect even today, hints that to people not brought up on literacy, the operation may be more than a little difficult. The difficulty is illustrated by the course which the development of writing took. The earliest efforts were pictures or pictographic writing. The significance here is that there was no connection between the visual symbol and the aural. The latter had been developed onomatopoeically or arbitrarily in a direct relationship with the thing or action or mood meant. Similarly, pictographs were developed originally in a direct and representational relationship with the thing or action meant. The symbol for the use of the eye tried to correspond to what the eye saw. The visual and aural symbols were each derived directly from the source of meaning and were independent of each other.

The arduous complexity and volume of pictographs probably limited their craft to a small number of people. Even this minority of craftsmen would have found such representation severely limited for the communication of sequences of thought, action, and nuance. It would be natural then for at least a few of the would-be communicators to work at devising some more effective mode of conveying meaning visually. Alternatively, some newcomers, possibly from another civilisation, might react against the several clumsinesses of the established mode and grope for something better. At any rate, as the representations were progressively attenuated into stylised signs, a technological breakthrough occurred. Somebody, about 5,000 years ago, tried attaching stylised, only quasi-representational symbols to the sounds of words, rather than to pictures of them. The visual medium was created directly for the oral medium rather than being modelled representationally from the thing or action. The symbol began to be divorced from the representation. Somehow the magical identity of the thing and the word for it was penetrated and it was realised, however inarticulately, that, if a set of sounds could represent a thing or an action or a tense on a pretty arbitrary basis, a set of visual signs might be similarly arbitrary. It was an early step in understanding the nature of language. But it stopped short of perceiving that each sounded word was itself composed from a relatively limited set of single sounds from combinations of which all the words of a given language were created. Nevertheless, the way for logographic writing was opened. A single artificial sign could now be made for every word. By that stroke, the representation of verbs, adjectives, adverbs was revolutionised and the possibilities of complex literature – as distinct from oral poetry and history – drew closer.

The trouble was the very number of words already in use. The original code-creators had to be infinitely ingenious in devising logographs to accommodate the language, while succeeding encoders and decoders required almost infinite memories to handle what was devised. The logographs were certainly an advance, but they were still clumsy. Another innovation was needed: eventually a modification was reached in the form of the logosyllabic scripts. These were a half-way house towards alphabets. They still attached a symbol to each word, but they recognised that the sounds of some words occurred as parts of the sounds of other words. Accordingly, a number of word signs were used also as syllables to form parts of other words. This constituted a significant economy. Although the scripts still required enormous effort and concentration for mastery, they were nevertheless manageable. Seven of these logosyllabic scripts are known and one of them, Chinese, survives till the present day. All of them seem to have endured through several centuries, so that their users quite clearly found them useful. The two earliest of them, Sumerian and Egyptian, overlapped well into the eras of the alphabetic scripts of Greek and Latin. Indeed, the Egyptian script seems to have fallen into disuse only about the time of the collapse of the Roman Empire, around A.D. 400–600.

Round about 1000 B.C., a good two millennia after the Sumerian logosyllabic script had established itself, some Phoenician or group of Phoenicians seems to have invented the first phonemic alphabet, albeit without vowel signs, and got it accepted in their community. In it, the sound value of a letter or combination of letters was totally independent of meaning. This, too, was a technological breakthrough, for it implied a fresh insight into the nature of spoken and written language. The fact that two millennia were needed before this new break occurred betokens first the satisfactory service of the logosyllabic scripts and second the psychological difficulty of perceiving words as composed of detachable parts

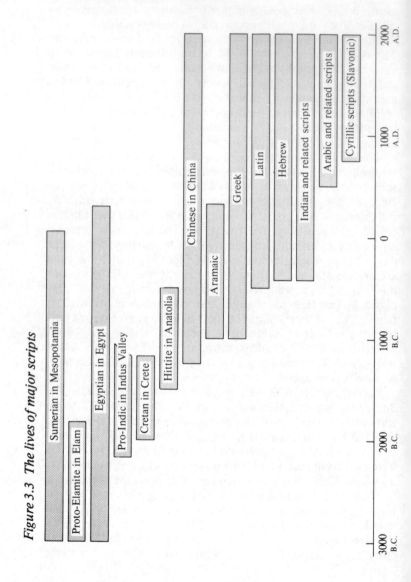

Figure 3.3 The lives of major scripts

which could be used elsewhere, and not as inviolable integers. That the break was accomplished not by the Mesopotamians or Egyptians, but by newcomers and outsiders, hints too at the forces for conservation and complacency, which may deter a society from improving the technologies at its disposal. The point is reinforced of course by the observation in the preceding paragraph, that the Egyptian script continued parallel with the Greek, and later the Latin, for well over a thousand years. This would call for no comment, if the three civilisations were not only almost adjacent, but interacted with sustained vigour economically and militarily. The Egyptian script had perhaps grown to be identified as part of a cultural heritage, too intimately woven into history, religion, government, commerce and literature to be changed for the sake of the conveniences of the scripts of new and upstart civilisations.

In what precisely did the breakthrough of the phonemic alphabet lie? It was the realisation that the words of a language are constructed from a small, commutable, inventory of sub-syllabic units, which the layman calls 'sounds', and which are our familiar consonants and vowels. (Technically, the linguist calls them phonemes.) In all languages, the number of consonant and vowel phonemes is remarkably smaller than the number of distinctive syllables, and these are of course very much fewer than the total of words in the language. In selecting the phoneme as the basis for the writing system, rather than the syllable or the word, the alphabetic innovators had discovered the most economic level at which to make the visual link with speech: one sign per phoneme, or distinctive speech-sound.

In the first place, then, the task for the memory would be materially lighter – the Greek alphabet, for instance, had only twenty-four letters, whereas the average person literate in Chinese would need to memorise between 4,000 and 5,000 different characters. It clearly followed that the skills of literacy would need less effort and exertion to learn, and would be a good deal less time-consuming; which in turn meant that more people would be able and would trouble to acquire them.

Conversely, because the code for a word now depended on its constituent sounds – and not on a stylised, wholly visual representation – it became possible to deduce spellings rather than having to rely totally on recalling them from memory. A writer – whether of books or of short memoranda – thus became freer and less burdened in his or her operation, being more able to work out a word, rather than have to look it up. Also, there was more leeway for spelling errors to occur without a loss of meaning: a reader could more easily make sense of misspelling, because he, too, could refer back to sounds and work out which word or words must have been intended by the writer. In this connection, it is relevant briefly to note the experience in Britain with the Initial Teaching Alphabet (i.t.a.) devised by Sir James Pitman. The purpose of the i.t.a. is, as its name suggests, to make the introduction to reading and writing in English easier for children.

It achieves an enormous gain in the consistency and reliability of spelling. For example, in ordinary English spelling the sound indicating the organ of sight, eye, can be indicated, 'My eye, I do like pie' – five spellings for the same sound. In the i.t.a., the same sentence would appear as 'Mie ie, ie du liek mie pie' – one symbol, one sound. Probably, because of this consistency, it was found that children launched on the i.t.a. and then transferred to ordinary script, tended to be better at spelling and, when they did make mistakes, made them logically, deducing spelling from sound. By contrast, children taught from the beginning in the ordinary script tended on average to be poorer at spelling and to make mistakes in a haphazard, illogical way. Expecting arbitrariness and inconsistency in the spelling, they seemed to abandon even the attempt to use their reason. The moral of this note is that alphabetic scripts probably do allow the reason more play, but on the other hand, they can actually hinder it, if they are allowed to become inconsistent and unpredictable to the beginner.

Third, it became possible to simplify the letters and make them wholly arbitrary. Whereas, in the early stages, the letters may have been based on some preceding drawn representation of some important word which began with the sound of a letter, this basis was in time forgotten and only the simple – and artificial – attachment of symbol to sound remained. Gradually, the letters could be streamlined and made much simpler both to write and to read than they could in logographic script. Again, access to literacy was facilitated.

In sum, by breaking words into their arbitrary assemblages of sounds and by attaching symbols to these sounds, the inventors and developers of the alphabet afforded the sense of hearing and the deductive reasoning much larger roles in literacy, without of course diminishing the importance of the sense of sight. And, while they did diminish the relative roles of the faculties of learning and memory in the mechanics of literacy, they left them freer to concentrate on the substance of what was being symbolised. Through using all the faculties involved in language more fully for literacy, the alphabet made the art of literacy more economical in its demands on human capacities and hence, more important, more accessible. Indeed, the alphabet made the possibility of universal literacy an easier feasibility in principle.

To underline the importance of the 'phonemic breakthrough' it is worth remarking that no similar step in the notation of language has occurred for nearly 3,000 years! The shorthands and mathematical languages which have sprung up in the last couple of centuries have been of vast value in supporting the advance of thought and technology, but remain very much the domain of a highly practised few. A short examination, say, of Pitman's shorthand will show that, while intensely economical, its conventions require more effort and memory than the everyday alphabet.

The potential for universal or, rather, mass literacy could not be exploited until relatively recently. Not until the invention of paper and printing in the fourteenth and fifteenth centuries A.D. was it possible to copy books, pamphlets and documents easily; and not until the advent of the powered press in the late eighteenth century was mass publication realised. Indeed, the 'paperback revolution' had to wait until the 1930s. Perhaps more important, however,

Figure 3.4 Examples of Chinese pictograms, ideograms, pictograms combined with phonetic elements, and homophones

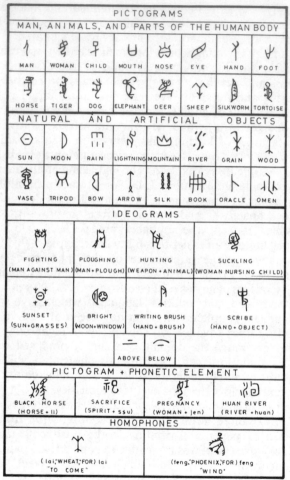

(Taken from David Diringer, *The Alphabet – A Key to the History of Mankind*, vol. 2, London, Hutchinson, 1968)

Figure 3.5 The 214 keys of Chinese writing

一丨丶丿乙亅 二亠人儿 10 入八冂冖冫 15 几凵刀力勹 20 匕匚匸十

卜 25 卩厂厶又 口 30 囗土士夂夊 35 夕大女子宀 40 寸小尢尸屮 45 山巛工

己巾 50 干幺广廴廾 55 弋弓彐彡彳 60 心戈戶手支 65 攴文斗斤方 70 无日

曰月木 75 欠止歹殳毋 80 比毛氏气水 85 火爪父爻爿 90 片牙牛犬 玄 95 玉

瓜瓦甘生 100 用田疋疒癶 105 白皮皿目矛 110 矢石示禸禾 115 穴立 竹米糸 120

缶网羊羽老 125 而耒耳聿肉 130 臣自至臼舌 135 舛舟艮色艸 140 虍虫血行衣 145

襾 見角言谷 150 豆豕豸貝赤 155 走足身車辛 160 辰辵邑酉釆 165 里 金長

門阜 170 隶隹雨青非 175 面革韋韭音 180 頁風飛食首 185 香 馬骨高髟 190 鬥

鬯鬲鬼 魚 195 鳥鹵鹿麥麻 200 黃黍黑黹黽 205 鼎鼓鼠鼻齊 210 齒龍龜龠 214

(From Diringer, *The Alphabet – A Key to the History of Mankind*)

Figure 3.6 From North-Semitic to modern caps

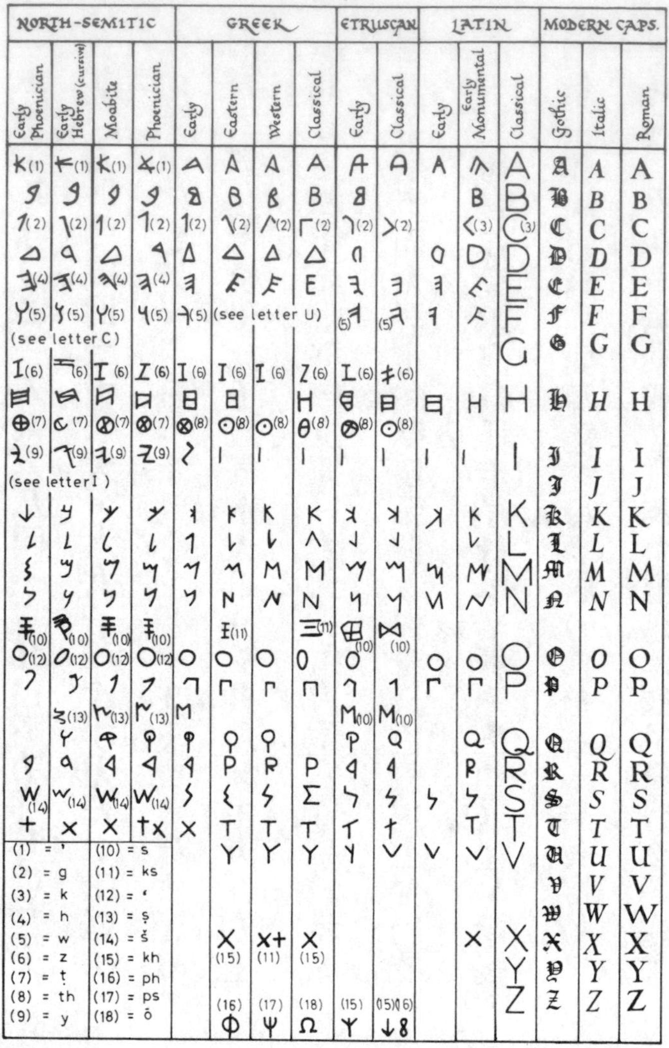
NORTH-SEMITIC
GREEK
ETRUSCAN
LATIN
MODERN CAPS.
Early Phoenician
Early Hebrew (cursive)
Moabite
Phoenician
Early
Eastern
Western
Classical
Early
Classical
Early
Early Monumental
Classical
Gothic
Italic
Roman
(see letter C)
(see letter U)
(see letter I)
(1) = '
(2) = g
(3) = k
(4) = h
(5) = w
(6) = z
(7) = ṭ
(8) = th
(9) = y
(10) = s
(11) = ks
(12) = ʿ
(13) = ṣ
(14) = š
(15) = kh
(16) = ph
(17) = ps
(18) = ō

(From Diringer, *The Alphabet – A Key to the History of Mankind*)

Figure 3.7 Development of the Arabic alphabet

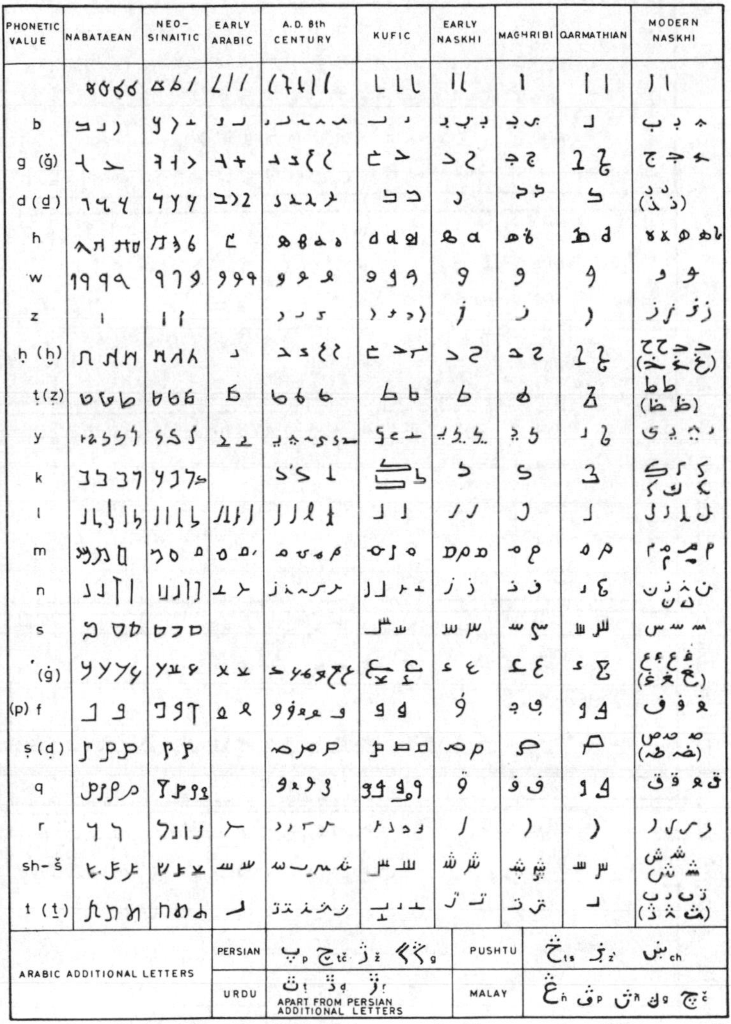

PHONETIC VALUE	NABATAEAN	NEO-SINAITIC	EARLY ARABIC	A.D. 8th CENTURY	KUFIC	EARLY NASKHI	MAGHRIBI	QARMATHIAN	MODERN NASKHI
b									
g (ǧ)									
d (ḏ)									
h									
w									
z									
ḥ (ḫ)									
ṭ (ẓ)									
y									
k									
l									
m									
n									
s									
' (ġ)									
(p) f									
ṣ (ḍ)									
q									
r									
sh – š									
t (ṯ)									

ARABIC ADDITIONAL LETTERS		PERSIAN			PUSHTU			
		URDU	APART FROM PERSIAN ADDITIONAL LETTERS		MALAY			

(From Diringer, *The Alphabet – A Key to the History of Mankind*)

Figure 3.8 Alphabet chart: Indian and Further-Indian scripts

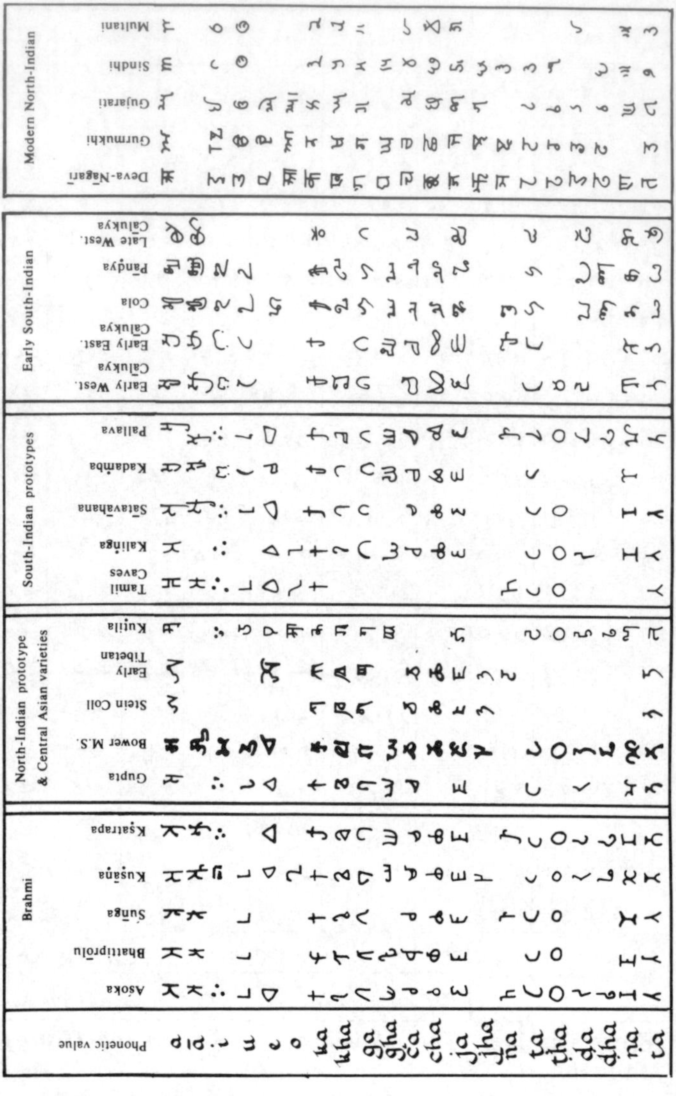

Phonetic value	Brahmi					North-Indian prototype & Central Asian varieties					South-Indian prototypes					Early South-Indian					Modern North-Indian				
	Asoka	Bhattiprolu	Sunga	Kushana	Ksatrapa	Gupta	Bower M.S.	Stein Coll	Early Tibetan	Kutila	Tamil Caves	Kalinga	Salavahana	Kadamba	Pallava	Early West Calukya	Early East Calukya	Cola	Pandya	Late West Calukya	Deva-Nagari	Gurmukhi	Gujarati	Sindhi	Multani
tha																									
da																									
dha																									
na																									
pa																									
pha																									
ba																									
bha																									
ma																									
ya																									
ra																									
la																									
va																									
sa																									
sa																									
sa																									
ha																									

(From Diringer, *The Alphabet – A Key to the History of Mankind*)

were the social forces sketched in the preceding chapter: commerce, technology, administration and religion. For it could be argued that, whatever the reading matter available, the ability to write could have been widely disseminated at any period, if there had been a sufficient concurrence of need, demand and diminution of opposition.

Specifying what literacy is and sketching its development do not of course explain its peculiar importance. In examining this, we need to recognise that we are entering areas which are not fully understood and which consequently are very controversial. Much of what will follow is speculative and in the nature of hypothesis. It is vulnerable to demolition, as research into various aspects of literacy is amplified. Part of the reason why so much is speculation is that the skills of literacy straddle several scientific disciplines, themselves in virtual infancy. Quite apart from the science of language, linguistics, the sciences of physiology and neurology need to be invoked to describe and understand the human mechanics of reading, understanding and writing. How, for instance, does the brain co-ordinate the visual and auditory abilities to produce meaning out of an assemblage of letters? That this is no idle question is illustrated by the phenomenon of hemialexia. Briefly, it has been found that after certain operations on the brain, people can have reading material presented to their left eye and be able to see it, but not read it, in the sense of being able to say what the material means. The same material, presented to their *right* eye, is both seen and read. There are also cases, again after certain brain operations, where a person is able to write, but not then able to read what he has written. Equally interesting is a finding among some Japanese who had sustained brain damage. These people had learned two forms of written language, one alphabetic, the other logographic. After suffering the damage, they could no longer read the alphabetic script, but still managed satisfactorily with the logographic. The interpretation might be that the ability of the brain to co-ordinate the auditory and visual senses had been destroyed, but not the ability to understand a purely visual code. (In passing, it can be remarked that, although the alphabet has brought great advantages, it may have had unexpected costs for a minority, perhaps very tiny, of unfortunate people. Also, of course, we may have lost some advantage through discarding the logosyllabic script.) Hence, an understanding of the neuroanatomy of literacy is a fundamental requirement for a complete understanding of the importance of literacy to the human being. However, the basis for such understanding is still only imperfectly assembled. Accordingly, it is still proper to speculate.

Neurology itself would not be enough, for it deals mainly with the mechanics. The science of psychology is necessary, too, for studying how individuals use and differ in their uses of their skills of literacy. How is it that some people, such as President John Kennedy, are able to read English at the rate of 1,000 words per minute, apparently with high comprehension, while most of us jog along at a modest 200–50 w.p.m.? How is it that most of us can learn to double our reading speeds very quickly and not lose any of our ability to comprehend what we are reading? Why are some people voracious readers, while others read only what they must, and even that reluctantly? How is it that some people pour out letters and books, while others can scarcely bear to scribble a Christmas card or two? Some of the answers to these questions may well lie within the individuals concerned. Yet some of them may have their roots less in the individual and more in his society. So that sociology is yet another science within the ambit of the study of literacy. For it will be recalled that literacy is a phenomenon created in response to an essentially social need, the need to communicate with others. It may also have been a response to a need to extend and reinforce the memory, but that, too, would have social functions. Certainly, the business accounts on the clay tablets of ancient Sumer were the product of human commerce – social and economic – grown too great to be held in the head of an individual.

In all three sciences, knowledge of literacy has not yet been pressed far enough to enable us to say we know all there is to know in any one science. Still less, of course, can we claim to have reached a satisfactory synthesis of the findings of the different sciences to enable us to erect a grand theory of the causes, processes and effects of literacy or different types of literacy. If we keep these severe limitations in mind, we may view the speculations which follow with a proper scepticism, yet with a modest openness also.

Let us return first to an earlier observation: literacy is a code of a code, a visual representation of an oral/aural means of communication, language. However, there is a difference between the two codes. Language is of course prior to literacy and the latter is dependent on the former. In addition, language can be argued to be part of the natural or genetic endowment of human beings. All human societies have language and every normal human child seems to learn language through innate mechanisms, which unfold in a kind of predictable programme.

We can assume for working purposes, that language is part of the normal equipment of the human being. Literacy, on the other hand, is not. It is an extension of language, true, but it is an artefact. For most of human history the human race has not possessed the skills of literacy. Even today, something like a third of the world's population and, as we have noted, in some states substantial majorities of people are illiterate. In some societies, literacy has even been lost. There is, however, an argument that literacy is as natural as language, so that it does not need to be taught formally. On the contrary, if it is not left to be learned as informally as language is learned by young children, its learning may actually be hampered. It is an argument with which the facts just listed are inconsistent. If some human beings possess literacy, while majorities or substantial minorities do not, then there can be nothing natural or instinctive in the acquisition of literacy. Children from houses in which much reading and writing are done may learn to read and perhaps to write, more or less on their own. Even so, these are extreme cases and can scarcely be used as a foundation for generalisation. On the evidence presently available, the working assumption of this book is that the skills and conventions of literacy have been deliberately invented and developed to assist memory and communication. Literacy, in short, is a technology, 'a technical method of achieving a practical purpose', if we may use the second of Webster's definitions.

The point in noting that literacy is a technology is to emphasise that it is the fruit of focused mental effort and reflection; it is not something that comes naturally. Inventing, developing, refining the arts of literacy exercised the faculties of a number of people. In the logographic scripts, for instance, inventing the symbols for abstract words with no immediate visual counterpart, creating mnemonics to facilitate learning, avoiding duplications and ambiguities between four or five thousand separate characters was not a task to be dashed off in one day by one person. There was, and there continues, an interaction or dialectic between the technical method and some of its users. (I had better explain in parenthesis that I use phrases like 'a number of people', 'some of the users', because it is evident that not all users of a technology – indeed, perhaps only a minute minority – use it with reflection and thought. Most users of a launderette, for instance, are content to stuff their clothes into a machine, put in the requisite detergents, press in a coin or two and leave the process of washing to itself. A washing-machine engineer, on the other hand, may watch the sequence of operations critically, with an eye to possible improvements and economies.) The importance of this dialectic is that it can spark changes not merely in the technology, but in the user as well. This observation is of course not confined to the technology of literacy; it applies, as the comparison with the washing machine implies, to all technology. When a human intelligence applies itself critically, reflectively and creatively to achieving a practical purpose, there is a potential – but only a potential – for achieving not only that purpose, but other things as well. It may spot another angle for tackling the problem marginally more efficiently; or it may light upon an insight which changes the entire technology, as the insight that letters could be attached directly to sounds revolutionised the technology of literacy; or it may have an idea which opens up new paths of thought and exploration quite separate from the purpose in hand.

The particular importance of literacy in the array of human technologies lies less in the technology itself and more in what it enables human intelligence to do. The ranges of scripts, print faces, calligraphy, arrangements of words on pages illustrate how the technology feeds on the psychology of perception and response in order to enhance and amplify communication. However, beyond this, the technology of literacy enables the human intelligence to interact with itself, to hone itself on itself. A person trying to puzzle out an argument, for instance, can write down the facts, the points, the possible relationships, the possible implications. He or she can then retrace the process of thought to detect flaws which need to be removed or areas where, say, additional facts need to be supplied. As Francis Bacon once put it: 'writing maketh an exact man'. By fixing thought in a stable, not immediately transitory, medium, a thinker renders it, so to speak, more within grasp, hence more controllable and malleable. The literacy of advanced mathematics is a supreme example of how thought and logic can be dissected and re-formed for the purpose of advancing thought. As with a mirror, the stable reflection of thought permits the thinker to contemplate the consequences and manipulate them. In controlling the expression of thought more consciously and critically, the thinker practises, and in practising strengthens, the power of thought. An obvious analogy is the development of the body's muscles through use and exercise. Thus literacy provides the ground both for strengthening the power of thought and for pushing thought beyond current boundaries. In addition, of course, working with the technology of literacy provides occasions for the flashes of inspiration and re-orientation of perspective and association which make for the sudden leaps in human thought. Literacy, as Jack Goody says, is the technology of the intellect (Goody, 1968).

What is possible for the individual thinker with his own thoughts is naturally also possible for a second thinker to do with the first thinker's work. Careful analysis and re-analysis of another person's information and deductions is not easily possible where only oral/aural communication obtains. The exact words and sequences of thought cannot be pinned in almost simultaneous focus or juxtaposed for closer comparison in ways that are possible with literacy. Literacy much more readily enables a second person to progress from the work of a first either by building on what the latter has done, that is by increment, or by incorporating the latter's work into his or her own, or by reacting sharply against it. Indeed, it has been said that academics write not for, but against, each other and that science progresses best by contradiction.

The two preceding paragraphs imply that the technology of literacy has served not simply the intended practical purposes of storing and communicating information. Vastly more important, it seems to have enabled the growth and development of the human reason and its power to combine different sources of information to produce even more understanding and inspiration. It has been potent, too, in the growth of self-consciousness and self-understanding.

This claim, however true, could of course affect only a very small minority of the thousands of millions of people who have acquired literacy in one language or another. Most men and women are not given to critical, reflective and creative uses of literacy. Most indeed find thinking itself sufficiently tiresome, without undertaking the added labour of organising it through reading and writing. Studies of almost universally literate societies – where nine or even ten years of compulsory schooling are administered to everybody, where public libraries, book production, magazines and newspapers are plentiful – suggest that only a minority of people spend more than a few minutes a day reading or writing outside the needs of their occupations. It seems to be the case also that many adults who complete literacy courses do not make much use of their laboriously acquired skills either because reading matter is not easily available or because the occasions for writing are infrequent. Relapses into illiteracy are apparently not uncommon.

If this is indeed so, what does it imply? Evidently, literacy takes different people differently: some use it to greater advantage than others. Would this suggest that it is misguided to regard literacy as a fundamental human right? It might better perhaps be regarded like the skills of carpentry or motor mechanics, to be learned only by those who want to learn them. The laws making it compulsory for every child to present itself for instruction in literacy and the efforts invested in adult literacy campaigns may be misplaced. In response to this line of argument, three points may be made.

In most societies today, the complexity of organisation and information is such that society could simply not continue without some form of literacy. In such societies, everybody at one time or another needs recourse to literacy for some purpose or another, and would be at a serious disadvantage without it. A simple example: how to read road signs in a strange town? Therefore, whatever the day-to-day use made of the skills, every member of such societies should have them at least handy for emergencies. In less complex societies, which run themselves satisfactorily without reliance on literacy, the question would obviously not be settled by this point.

The second response is that we have no way of telling beforehand those who will use literacy to push the frontiers of thought and technology further, those who will need the skills for intensive daily application, those who will use them casually, and those who will let them rust altogether. We might well be able to talk in terms of probabilities: a woman who comes from a poor rural family in an isolated nomadic tribe will be much more likely to relapse into illiteracy than the son of a professor at a British university. Even so, we could not talk in terms of certainties. The skills of literacy are so important to human mental development, the need for 'frontier pushers' so permanent, the possibility of discovering such people in 'deprived' or 'primitive' communities so far from negligible, that the opportunities for literacy should be rationed only for the gravest of reasons.

The third consideration is more in the form of a question.

Is it possible that a major effect of literacy lies not in the use of the skills *after* they are acquired, but actually in the process of acquiring them? Earlier we mentioned Napoleon's irascibility with illiterate recruits, who could not learn to regulate the length of their pace. He seemed to suppose a connection between their slowness and clumsiness and their lack of schooling and illiteracy. Was he right?

Testing the plausibility of the suggestion requires that we trace what is normally required for anyone to learn to read and write. (We ought to note here that whatever is done in learning reading and writing may also be done in learning other operations. Hence, no properties exclusive to literacy are being suggested: they might well be achieved through learning something else.) Because there are different methods of teaching reading and writing, it is not possible to trace a single order of instruction and learning. Nevertheless, the substantive steps are identical, even if the sequence in which they are taken may vary. And we should note that we assume we are dealing with a phonetic alphabet.

From the first lesson in reading, there starts an awareness – more conscious perhaps in adult learners than among children – that language is a convention. The structure and mechanics begin to show themselves and to bring about the realisation that language is not an arbitrary endowment, but a creation with system, regularities and rules: it is something within the learner's control, over which he can have power. A new perspective on a familiar tool is being achieved. It is a step towards mastering the environment rather than only responding to it.

Part of this is a recognition of words as entities in themselves, separable from particular contexts. Another part is the realisation that words, too, can be broken into separable sounds; that these sounds can be recombined into any number of other words within the knowledge of the learner.

There is also a realisation, which forms gradually, that a mark, meaningless in itself and representing nothing visible, can represent a sound, also in itself meaningless; and can be combined with other marks to create meaning. The manipulable nature of literacy and the ability of the literate to manipulate it are part of the concepts of control.

More mechanically, but also important, is the fine training of the eye. The reader needs to know and to recognise all the letters in the alphabet. Further, he needs to know them well enough to be able to tell them apart, when they are juxtaposed. While this may seem a trivial task to the practised reader, it takes the beginner time and patience. For instance, in the English and similar alphabets, the letters 'b', 'd', 'p', 'q', 'l', 't', 'f' can cause difficulty of recognition and reading. The visual discrimination required is finer than the normal needs of everyday life and is consequently sharpening and extending a skill.

Similarly, learning to read and write calls the memory into play – less so in phonetic scripts than in logosyllabic of course, but that is only a matter of degree. The important point is that the use of the memory is not casual or random, but a matter of deliberate and systematic effort, a calculated extension of a faculty. It may strike one as a trifle paradoxical that, while literacy is an adjunct to the memory for storing information and indeed can relieve the memory of having to hold quantities of only occasionally used data, its own exercise depends partly on a careful training of the memory. A frequent assertion has it that the memories of illiterate people are more capacious and retentive than those of literates. The corollary would be that dependence on literacy might actually involve the under-development of the memory, if not its atrophy. The evidence for the claim is based usually on the oral historians and story-tellers of illiterate societies, of whom the wandering minstrels of ancient Greece, singing thousands of lines of the *Iliad* and *Odyssey* by heart, are a classic instance. No systematic evaluation of this claim seems to be available and it is countered by impressions that illiterate people both take longer to learn new operations and forget what they have learned more quickly. For instance, one group attempting to train illiterate farmers through oral instructions found that no farmer was able to remember a sequence of operations in its entirety (Anderson and

Bowman, 1966). It will be recalled, too, that managers in copper mines thought that their illiterate workers seemed to forget their training rather rapidly, when they returned to their villages on leave.

Perhaps more important than the sheer exercise of the memory is the necessity of coupling the memory with intelligent application. Until it becomes so fast as to be almost automatic, reading is never a simple act of recognition or memory. When a reader looks at a word he has never seen before, he has to 'attack' it, to break it into its letters and syllables, rebuild it into sounds and then extract its meaning. The process is naturally easier to observe with beginning than with skilled readers. It brings into intelligent, not automatic, play a number of faculties. If this is true of single words, it is obviously much truer of sentences, paragraphs and chapters. In reading these, the reader not only has to recognise or remember all the words from past encounters, but has also to hold them in his short-term memory, until the whole sense becomes clear. In the early stages of reading, when the beginner has to analyse and reconstitute almost every word in a passage, the process is laborious, not to say painful. Quite often, at the end of a relatively short sentence, the beginner will be unable to say what the sentence said, even though every word has been correctly deciphered. Similarly, until a speed of reading is attained, sufficient to permit the memory to hold meaning for the required span, beginners can find it difficult to understand a story. This means that the memory is being mobilised and stretched to help the intelligence attain understanding. There is in fact a complex process of dynamic mental co-ordination, not only being undertaken deliberately, but also being pushed to a more and more rapid and efficient pitch of performance. The activity in itself would be exercising and thus toning both the physiological and psychological mechanisms involved.

Concomitantly, the mechanisms which are involved in the process of learning will be similarly exercised. The ability to concentrate will perforce be developed because the individual sessions will demand attention, spanning periods from forty minutes to two hours; and because the sessions will be spread over many months, demanding discipline and perseverance. Underlying this effort and perhaps not even noticed, even though experienced, will be the notion of systematic learning, planned and sequenced, so that each item of learning is built upon a predecessor and prepares the ground for a successor. (Naturally, the impact of such a notion will depend upon the quality of the course and instruction undergone.)

The total effect of these various exercises and efforts, if taken to a sufficient degree, may so change the quality and outlook of a mind, that some kind of transformation or awakening can be said to have occurred. (Here we really are in the realm of speculation and uncertainty.) If a physiological analogy may be taken again: people who embark on jogging or other exercises to maintain their physical fitness may outwardly appear unchanged. Yet within themselves they feel better, more vigorous, functioning more efficiently, more fitted for flexible response to new situations. Similarly, the persistent and strenuous exercise of the faculties in learning to read may raise a person to a better level and wider range of mental functioning. That in itself would be a gain, even if a person did not read much afterwards.

So far, only the skills of reading have been considered. Those of writing are different and for most people a good deal more difficult. Adult literacy programmes demonstrate the fact clearly. For instance, UNESCO in its Work Oriented Adult Literacy Programmes in Iran and Tanzania found that what primary-school children could attain in reading in about four years, could be attained by adults in less than half the time. As for writing, however, the adults could in the same period of learning reach only what primary-school children were managing after their second year. Put crudely, it appears that writing is about twice as hard as reading for adults. An independent project in Turkey came to the same conclusion. It was almost impossible to predict attainment in writing from attainment in reading: good readers could be relatively poor writers. On the other hand, reading attainment could be predicted with almost certainty from writing attainment: good writers were practically sure to be good readers. The reasons for this are not difficult to conjecture: a tracing of the steps in writing will clarify them.

Let us assume a writer – female or male, though the masculine pronoun is used – who is writing spontaneously, that is, neither copying what someone else has written nor taking dictation. To start, he needs to have some idea of what he wants to express. It might be possible to put out his thoughts in just the same way as he would have spoken them, or it might be necessary to be careful and hence to put some thought into composing the right sentences. The thoughts or feelings require then to be transposed into words. The words have to be converted into letters, which need to be selected, at least, *almost* correctly selected, if the reader is to understand clearly what is intended. In a perfect alphabetic script, the spellings of the words can be worked out, if they are imperfectly remembered. In an imperfect and inconsistent alphabetic script, like that we have for English, greater reliance has to be placed on memory; while in the case of a logographic or logosyllabic script, the role of memory and mnemonics will be even larger. Then consideration of syntax and correct expression may need to be taken into account. These are of minor importance, where there are small differences between the spoken and written languages. However, where there exist a literary or 'high' language and a demotic, popular or vulgar spoken language or dialect, the matter may loom large in the mind of the writer and even exercise an inhibiting effect. Having marshalled his thoughts and words, the writer has then to convert them into intelligible marks on paper or other writing material. The more advanced writer may use a typewriter or similar machine to undertake the conversion: if he is expert at the machine, he will be able to transfer his words piecemeal through all eight fingers and at least one of two thumbs – a feat of well-developed psychomotor co-ordination. The ordinary writer will normally use some form of pen or pencil and the thumb and two fingers of one hand in order to shape the necessary marks. If he is well practised, he will write fairly rapidly in a cursive script which economises in movements of the hand. If, on the other hand, he is a beginner, he will probably print each letter separately, sounding each out to himself as he goes along. For the practised writer, making the necessary marks can become so routine, automatic and fast, that his script can degenerate almost into illegibility. For the beginning writer, making the marks can be so great an effort that he can hardly hold the letters compactly into easily recognisable words, much less hold them in a line, whether a guiding line is available or not. (The difficulties would of course be compounded by the complexity of a given script: the Turkish script probably gives its learners less trouble than the Chinese.) The reason is that the psychomotor co-ordination required to get the eye and fingers to trace the desired shapes is much finer than is needed for most of the operations of everyday life. (Such an observation would not, of course, be true of occupations like needle-work or embroidery, but is more plausible in the cases of farming or carpentry and most unskilled work.) Learning such co-ordination later in life tends to demand much effort and application.

As with reading, perhaps as important as achieving this co-ordination is the sustained concentration of the intelligence, that is a pre-requisite for it. The human system may through this perseverance reach a new level of ability to learn and to co-ordinate itself. The ramification or repercussion leads to learning more easily than other operations which may call for keen psychomotor co-ordination. Perhaps Napoleon was right: soldiers who have been systematically drilled, pushed and stretched into being good readers and writers, need much less drilling – i.e. learn more rapidly – the tedious routines of the army.

That is to say – to return to our third response – the very process of becoming literate is valuable to the learner, whether or not he makes much use of the skills of literacy afterwards. It may then be asked why this particular form of learning or training should be raised over others to the status of a basic human right which every state is obliged to enable its citizens to acquire. A first guess could be that there must exist an intuitive conviction that the human brain and intelligence are the 'crown of all creation', as we know it; that survival and progress depend on their continued development; so that any activity or skill which promotes this as obviously as does literacy, should be encouraged, even enforced.

This intuition has been reinforced in the past two decades by research into the effects of literacy upon individuals. As was indicated in the previous chapter, there appear to be strong indications that attainments in literacy are associated with dispositions favourable towards planned change in a society. In less hedged terms, it would seem that the more literate people are, the more willing they are to accept and work for improvements in their societies. Their sense of 'personal efficacy' is increased: that is, they gain confidence that they are able to do something about their own lives, they are not merely pawns in the control of greater forces. They acquire stronger convictions about physical, rather than magical, causality; planning the future seems more possible. They become more willing to reason for themselves, less willing to take opinions on authority, and therefore apparently more willing to participate in voluntary organisations and politics. The wider experiences made available through reading materials enable people to be less parochial and less intolerant of cultures different from their own. Literacy in short appears to be an important element in the process of modernising a society through the cumulation of changes in the abilities and outlook of its individual citizens.

At the same time, it would be incautious not to remark that the changes in outlook associated with literacy may be less the effects of literacy as such, and more the effects of the people who conduct the schools, organise literacy programmes, write the text-books and distribute reading materials. If these people, through the medium of teaching and promoting reading and writing, simultaneously promote changes of attitude and habit – as they usually do – then the total credit cannot be accorded to the psychomotor changes induced by the operations of reading and writing. We have always to bear in mind that there have been literate social groups, who so far from being inventive and thrusting, have been content merely to copy their ancient scriptures and pass them on virtually unaltered. It may be, then, that literate people can respond more readily to leadership for change in culture, technology, social mores, but that literacy by itself does not induce appetites for change, improvement or exploration.

While the drift so far has been to point to the beneficial effects of literacy and acquiring literacy on the individual, there is a strand of thought which warns that the forms in which literacy is embodied, may have unexpected limiting effects upon the human being. Precisely because an important technology emphasises certain operations and calls upon certain faculties, other faculties may recede into disuse and even atrophy. More subtly, because such a technology calls on the faculties involved to work in only a certain way, it may discourage more varied uses and developments: it can act as a blinker. These sorts of possibilities have been eloquently, if dogmatically, explored by Marshall McLuhan in *The Gutenberg Galaxy* (1962) but remain questions for research and verification. However, we may examine the plausibility of one or two of his ideas.

There is, for example, the tendency for the reader to become merely a receiver rather than a reactor. Although the intelligence and reason have to be used in reading something, the fact that they are preoccupied in taking something in can inhibit their treating it to a critical assessment. The imputed authority of the printed word is evidenced by the well-known and frequent exhortation that we should not believe all we see in print. While it is probably a hangover from the times when literacy was not widespread and books were written mainly by the learned, the facts that it still needs to be watched and that schools and universities have deliberately to stimulate critical approaches to literature of all kinds, warns that reading can retard the development of the intellect. The notion sounds plausible enough. Yet immediately it raises the question why some people react critically to print, while others act as simple receivers. Is the issue less a matter of the effect of literacy on the intelligence in general and more a matter of how a particular reader has been previously trained? Perhaps the ratio of critical to 'credulous' readers in a given community or society is the outcome of a dialectic between certain particularly thoughtful individuals and prevailing social values. If the society is authoritarian, rewards conformity and is at best wary of questioners, then the likelihood of the majority of readers being credulous would presumably be high. If, on the other hand, the questioners have succeeded in persuading large numbers of their fellow citizens that an independent, critical and questing stance is much to be valued, the proportions of questioning readers would likely grow. (The dependence of the use of literacy on social norms is a topic to which we shall return in the next chapter.)

A second topic of musing is the differences between what is called a Manuscript culture and our present Print culture. McLuhan points out that, when books had all to be written by hand, the scripts tended to reflect speech: words were not separated from each other by spaces, but ran continuously one into another. Although present-day readers might find this style discommoding – initially, at least – readers of the Manuscript cultures appear not to have been handicapped. They read aloud to themselves and to each other, and thus in script and decoding maintained an overt connection between speech and literacy. And because everything had to be written by hand, a kind of union and balance was maintained between the auditory, visual, tactile and enunciatory faculties. None was emphasised at the expense of the others.

The advent of print changed this relationship. Most obviously, words were printed separate from each other, no longer running together. The tendency to take things apart, to individualise, to specialise, received a weight in its favour. As McLuhan puts it, 'Print exists by virtue of the static separation of functions and fosters a mentality that gradually resists any but a separative and compartmentalising or specialist outlook' (p. 126). Part of the separating and specialising tendency was manifested in the rise of the printers' trade: writers now needed to depend much more openly on printers and became to a lesser extent producers of their works. True, they wrote the books and poems, but they no longer distributed handwritten copies of them. True, too, they might take pleasure in the printed products, but the tactile relationship between them and their readers or audience was replaced by a mechanical one. Further, as the volume of print increased over the centuries, reading aloud grew less and less to be the habit, until nowadays it is used only for social occasions, like bed-time stories or church services. The reader who reads aloud to himself is deemed to be inefficient. Similarly, techniques to accelerate reading speeds depend in part on eliminating as far as possible the auditory element of the print: readers are urged not to let words sound themselves even mentally. The visual faculty is consequently stressed as the sole communicator to the intelligence, while those of touch, hearing and enunciation are excised. The union and balance are destroyed. Since literacy is so important to the individual in a highly literate society, a kind of lopsided development or evolution may be incipient.

Again, there is plausibility in the thesis. Even so, a certain sense of proportion seems called for. Whatever the harmony, union and balance perpetrated by the Manuscript culture, they remained precisely because of the limitations of the manuscript, the property and privilege of very small minorities of people. Often this privilege was deliberately reserved and restricted to specialised groups of people, like a priestly caste. On the other hand, whatever the imbalances engendered by print, its advantages are at least accessible to much vaster proportions of the human race. If it is true that the very acquisition of the skills of literacy entail an enhancement of intellectual and psychomotor skills, then print, which at least permits universal acquisition, is to be welcomed.

More extremely, it might be argued that, while this balance of the senses may indeed have been of value from the stance of aesthetics, the other side of its coin may have been the encouragement of pleasing sound and pleasing script at the expense of worthwhile meaning – a developmental cul-de-sac for language, literacy and the individual intelligences concerned. Further, it may be misguided to see permanent value in an equilibrium of the senses, which may have been essentially temporary and transient in the development of a technology.

Finally, of course, it needs to be pointed out that literacy is not the only technology with which the senses of man interact. While literacy in its present usage may indeed stress the visual faculties, other technologies may call into play the auditory, enunciatory, tactile, olfactory and other faculties. They are not likely to wither for want of exercise. It may be that a technology which mobilises several faculties at once is for that reason to be preferred over one which uses only one or two. However, if the latter better suits the practical purpose for which a technology is needed in the first place, a decision to forgo the former may be wise.

Yet a point needs to be made on the other side. Certain communications – reports, for instance – do want to transmit only information and are essentially indifferent to tone, colour and subtlety. An individual would evidently be efficient to adapt his reading skills to extract the maximum meaning for the minimum outlay of effort and time. If such an adaptation meant restricting his reading only to the visual element of the report, well and good. On the other hand, much literature – poetry and many novels, for instance – wants to transmit not only information, but, much more, intimations of emotions, resonances of ambiguities with one word or a combination of them, excitements of new understanding. For such literature, the sounds and tones of language are of equal importance with the visual signal. If a reader were to depend solely on the latter, he would be inefficient, because part of the intended communication would be lost. Speed-reading would in effect be an inappropriate adaptation of a technology for the practical purpose at hand.

A last proposition we shall consider is that the technology of print works to impair the human memory. Memory functions not simply by grasping disparate points of experience, but also by arranging some of them in associated groups: when one item in the group is touched or located, it can trigger the memorisation of the rest. If the memory can grasp some of the senses in a mnemonic, it reinforces its capacity to recall given experiences. For easy example, the smell of frying chips can recall a mother and a kitchen at a given moment of a person's life, besides evoking fish and chip shops as well. Similarly, then, if the memory can group the visual, auditory and tactile senses in reading something, it reinforces itself and so is more likely to remember what it has read. If, on the other hand, only the visual sense is used in reading a memorandum, the likelihood of forgetting is increased, because the memory can utilise no ready means of reinforcement. Hence, the more speed-reading or similar techniques are used, the more impaired is the memory. To that proposition could be added another: print has made it so easy to store and to retrieve information, that the very need and incentive to remember has been weakened. Consequently, even if the memory itself is not impaired, in the sense of being unable to function normally, neither is it being encouraged to develop to its full potential.

The strength and importance of these propositions are difficult to assess. It could be argued that those who are moved to adopt techniques which eliminate the auditory and tactile elements from reading, are under pressure to read much. Even if they retained more than the visual elements, they could not possibly remember all they read. Accordingly, it is the more rational choice to cover more and remember what is needed selectively and deliberately, than to cover less and to remember involuntarily what may not be useful. Second, to recall a previous argument, literacy is not the only technology to require that a person use his memory. That a person uses his memory less for reading does not automatically impair the memory for other purposes. In regard to the second proposition, it can be pointed out that a purposive search for needed information is probably more likely to result in useful retention by the memory, than a random collection of information, which only might prove to be useful. And again it does not require literacy exclusively to enable a person to develop his memory to the full; other means are either available or can be devised.

The main thread of this chapter has been the attempt to explain why literacy is given such a very special place among the technologies invented by mankind. In crude terms of biological and psychological evolution, it seems to have been the major means whereby the human brain and intelligence have enabled themselves to develop concepts both to interpret and capitalise on the phenomena around them and to acquire further knowledge, understanding and technologies. Even where literacy has not been used for such purposes, the very process of acquiring it demands such effort and results in such psychomotor attainments, that its learners seem to reach a level of mental operation not available to the average illiterate. This attainment may make them more responsive to leadership for change in various spheres, but may not cause them to become readers themselves.

Further reading

David Diringer (1968) (3rd edn.), *The Alphabet – A Key To The History of Mankind*, London, Hutchinson, 2 vols.

John Downing, ed. (1975), *Comparative Reading: Cross-National Studies of Behaviour and Processes in Reading and Writing,* New York, Macmillan.

I. J. Gelb (1963) (2nd edn), *A Study of Writing*, University of Chicago Press.

John T. Guthrie, ed. (1976), *Aspects of Reading Acquisition,* Baltimore, Johns Hopkins University Press.

Alex Inkeles and David H. Smith (1974), *Becoming Modern,* London, Heinemann.

Marshall McLuhan (1962), *The Gutenberg Galaxy*, London, Routledge & Kegan Paul.

J. D. N. Versluys (1977), 'What Does A Literacy Course Achieve?', pp. 569–99 in *Teaching Reading And Writing To Adults: A Sourcebook*, Tehran, International Institute For Adult Literacy Methods.

Chapter four
Literacy and society

So far we have looked at the distribution of literacy through-
out the world and inside particular societies, at the conditions
under which literacy flourishes, at the possible effects that
acquiring literacy might have on the psychology of the individual, the possibilities opened by literacy and – but only lightly
– at the reasons why such possibilities are often not realised.
Now we shall move from the individual back to society, which
is to say to the individual in association with other individuals
either in relatively small groups or in large masses. Our
purpose will be to explore why it is that different societies
seem to make very different uses of literacy.

A recurring phenomenon in history is that literacy appears
to flourish, when large, complex states and cities are
organised together with a good deal of craft, industry and
trade. This seems to have been the case with the cities and
states of ancient Mesopotamia, going back to Ur and Sumer,
of ancient Egypt, of Crete, of the Achaean or Mycenaean
civilisation in Greece which collapsed round 1200–1100 B.C.,
of the Greek civilisation which succeeded it four or five
centuries later, and of ancient China. Small-scale civilisations, whether sedentary – like the islanders of Fiji – or
shifting – like the tribes of Central Africa – or nomadic, like
the Touareg of North Africa or the Masai of East Africa, do
not appear to create literacy for themselves, very possibly
because they simply do not need it. Life and business,
exchange and commerce, are all manageable without it. On
the other hand, operations on a large scale, with many transactions being undertaken by single individuals, begin to tax
the memory, so that some form of record and storage of
information becomes necessary. Particularly is this so, when
different steps in a transaction take place over relatively long
periods of time.

To phrase the matter in this fashion implies that record and storage were the first functions of literacy – and with the majority of people who learned literacy in its early appearances, perhaps the only functions. It should not imply, however, that the sphere of these functions was restricted only to commerce and other business transactions. The use of the technology for other spheres was rapidly perceived, not least for the laws, the administration of state, and the monuments of vainglorious kings. Hamurabi, king of Babylon about 1800 years before Christ, had the laws of his land engraved upon a pillar, so that all could read what was forbidden and what the likely punishment for transgression was. Another early use of literacy was the listing of royal appointments, rather like a government gazette, so that all should know who had – and who had not – royal authority for his actions. The function of recording applied, too, to poetry and song, for the first tasks were to write down epics created generations earlier and handed down from bard to bard orally, doubtless with additions, modifications and losses. The *Iliad* of Homer, for instance, although created round a war which occurred in the twelfth century B.C., was not written down till perhaps the middle of the eighth century B.C.

Going beyond recording and using literacy for communicating information, instructions, requests or negotiations was again an early step. We know, for instance, that the kings of Mesopotamia and Egypt sent letters to each other along with their embassies and loads of gifts. Again it seems to have arisen as a response to a need.

As a response – in so far as concerned recording, storing, and communicating information – literacy would have followed, not preceded, the formation of certain kinds of society. It would have been, then, not a prerequisite to their formation, although it might well have become a necessary condition of their continuance and expansion. On the contrary, without such formations, literacy would not have been created. In the previous chapter, it will be recalled, we discussed the drive for literacy as though it might be a pre·

requisite not only to the rapid formation of industrial trading states, like those we know today, but also to the intellectual and technological advance of the human intelligence. Are these interpretations inconsistent or might both be true? It may be that literacy is both contingent on certain forms of society and a necessary condition for certain forms of intellectual advance. Let us pursue this latter supposition a little further.

It does seem to be true that some literate civilisations have contributed much to man's knowledge and understanding of the world and the forces around him. The Mesopotamians laid the foundations of mathematics: the bridge which Pythagoras built for asses was discovered by the Mesopotamians a millennium earlier, as an inscription now in Baghdad demonstrates clearly. The Egyptians were known for their astronomy as well as their astrology. The Greeks of Ionia and the mainland developed logic, scientific thought and philosophy much further than others seem to have managed to do earlier, or even later. As far as we know, no illiterate civilisation has matched these achievements, even though they may have considerable attainments of their own; as for example, Polynesian navigation across the Pacific Ocean. It is not implausible to suppose then that the association between literacy and intellectual and scientific advance is close.

On the other hand, it cannot help but be noted that the advances of the literate civilisations were not ceaseless. Eventually stagnation seems to set in and originality to be replaced by ornament, and what has been called 'clichéd thought'. The Greeks, for instance, were dazzling during the sixth, fifth and fourth centuries B.C., but later did not improve much upon their achievements. They seem to have been content to hark back to them or embroider upon them, but not to push them further. The same could be said of the contented literati of China and India, who certainly possessed and wrote books, but who appear not to have been at all thrusting in their use of literacy. In Kerala, in South India, prior to the coming of the British, several different groups were literate in a number of different scripts, but they did not astonish the world with new advances. Rich young men in Burma were sent to learn to read and write, but apparently only for the gratification of having done so: it was an ornamental achievement, neglected and dropped once attained. Two tribes in Madagascar are known to have had the Arabic script for several centuries, but to have done very little with it. Similarly, the Tibetans have long had a vast reverence for books and writing, going so far indeed as to paint prayers upon water. And yet they have advanced the art in so meagre a fashion as to be accused of grapholatry. The mediaeval Christian monks who so laboriously copied out the manuscripts of the scriptures and other literature might be put in the same class. Assiduous copying, garnished with more and more elaborate and colourful calligraphy, could well be regarded and valued as achievements in preserving knowledge and ideas and in fine aesthetics – not only in Europe, but in China, Japan, Persia, India and other places, too; but it does not seem to have lifted the copiers themselves into new realms of speculation or science. (Indeed, one might argue that copying by hand, like copying by typewriter, diverts attention so completely from the substance of the language to the shape of the letters, from the whole piece to its minute components, that it is more likely to deaden than to enliven the intelligence, and so to suffocate rather than provoke thought and reflection.)

It appears, then, that literacy depends for its emergence on certain formations of society (and can be extinguished, if these formations disappear); it accompanies periods of intellectual and technological advance, but it also coexists with periods of intellectual stagnation and decline. If the case is indeed so, it would follow that, if intellectual advance is not possible without literacy, then literacy may be a necessary condition, but is clearly not sufficient for it. If we revert to the notion of literacy as a technology, we can hazard the beginning of a general explanation of this possibility.

All tools are designed to meet a need – or possibly a set of needs. If that need recedes or disappears, the tool will be neglected or lie in disuse. Further, the tool will tend to be restricted by its original users to the purpose for which it was created. However, new situations may arise, which uncover wider applications for the tool. More important, people other than the original users may detect uses for purposes of their own. According to this scheme, literacy may well have been created simply as an aid to memory for businessmen and merchants. Administrators and priests – often the same people in societies of priest-kings – would have taken it up for their own needs for records and references. Then its uses for communications between businessmen and between officials would have become apparent – although the actual embodiment may have restricted its use. For instance, when clay tablets were the main medium for records and messages, long letters and arguments would have been cumbersome to transmit and clearly vulnerable to breakage: the incentive to brevity would have been powerful. The step from mere communication to the development of logic and science would have been largely the undertaking of people who were possibly neither businessmen nor officials, but men of strong intellectual curiosity with sufficient economic support not to have to devote most of their time to earning a livelihood. They may have used literacy simply to jot down notes, as an aid to their memory, and from there almost indeliberately began to use it – through revision, the removal of inconsistencies, the honing to greater precision – as a tool for thinking and logic. They might not have perceived at first that they were transforming literacy from a mere means of record to a stimulus and support for fresh thought, argument, research and discovery.

The next step is to speculate as to the conditions in which people of 'strong intellectual curiosity' might flourish. An assumption implicit in the last paragraph was that wealth and leisure were necessary. Yet the list of examples of intellectually stagnant societies was composed almost exclusively of those which contained groups with both leisure and sufficient means to live. Evidently, then, wealth and leisure may, like literacy, be necessary conditions, but they, too, even in combination with literacy, are not sufficient. More exploration is required. The answer is likely to be a complicated combination of circumstances recurring in several quarters, a series of interactions between individual personalities, their particular positions in their societies, the intimate groups surrounding them, the norms and institutions of their larger society, the inventions, discoveries and adventurous hypotheses within and beyond their society, and their encounters with other societies of different cultures and perspectives. Throwing all these factors into one sentence makes them rather a mouthful to digest, but at least underlines three points. The first is that we are dealing with a social phenomenon and hence must look for a network of not necessarily equally reciprocating influences and must not hope for a single explanation. The second is that interactions involve stimuli, either encouraging or deterrent, and responses, eager, uninterested or hostile. The third, more latent, is that an absence of stimulus may have consequences quite as important as an abundance of it.

Let us begin this exploration not from the individual's perspective, but from that of a society, some groups of which have recently developed or adopted the technology of literacy. These groups – merchants, administrators, priests – would take up the technology in order to meet their own needs and would, at least in the first instance, be little concerned with the needs of others. Reciprocally, those who were aware of the technology but saw no particular application of it in their own callings and stations in life, would probably not bother to acquire it themselves. The needs of the innovating groups would probably correspond to the first function of writing, making notes in order to preserve and to recall. In this sense, they would be *conserving* information, knowledge, norms and instructions. Literacy would be employed as an innovation to help do the same, only better, and to conserve the *status quo* – by no means to embark on adventure, let alone revolution. The society in general being only partially affected by literacy, would have changed little in its mentality, outlook or processes. It would continue to live by the accepted norms, to value conformity, to respect established authority and tradition and its modes of education and learning would continue to be mainly oral, from teacher to pupil, from master to disciple, from crafts-man to apprentice. In its social organisation, the *status quo* would more than likely be specialised and hierarchical (we may recall that literacy appears almost exclusively in complex and developed urban societies). Specialisation means not only that there would be craftsmen, artisans and professionals like lawyers and doctors, but also that there would be experts and authorities in certain limited areas, dependent for their living and status on their expertise. Hierarchy means that some persons and groups of persons would have more responsibility, status, influence, power – and possibly more wealth, also – than others, and less of all these things than yet others. A few would be pre-eminent on some or all counts and would be regarded as leaders or members of the ruling classes. Both specialisation and hierarchy would generate interests vested in the perquisites and advantages of a professional and political authority. To the extent that literacy secured those interests, it would be welcomed by them. In so far as it appeared to threaten them with dilution or diminution – e.g., priests having their interpretations of a holy book challenged – literacy might well be restricted, resisted or even suppressed.

For example, the priests who safeguarded and taught the body of religious knowledge, ritual and custom would probably welcome the writing down of all they carried in their heads. While it might not immediately lessen what they had to learn to be initiated into the priesthood, it would provide recourse for refreshment and verification. On the other hand, they would probably not welcome their books being made available to the general public: their grounds would be several. Overtly, they would argue that the holy books were not open books, but couched in terms which were obscure, ambiguous and liable to dangerous misunderstanding. The faithful should, for their own good, continue to rely on oral interpretation and the instruction of those schooled in the true meaning of wisdom.

Examples of such a stance can of course be quoted from Egyptian, Hebraic, Christian and Islamic times. Socrates and Plato were apparently in agreement; they felt that as the written word could not be interrogated and answer back, it was a poor amd misleading medium of instruction and learning. In A.D. 1543, King Henry VIII of England issued an edict forbidding labourers to read the Christian Bible, even though the general trend of the Reformation was to make the Bible as widely available as possible.

Less openly and perhaps not even admitted to themselves, the priests would wish to counter a change which might bring their religious and moral authority into question and debate.

One step further along, a diminution of authority might raise the issue of redundancy together with the loss of professional status and livelihood. (That such fears might be proved groundless in the long run, would not be apparent in the early stages. Such fears would also be more forceful in societies where alternative congenial employments were scarce and where supportive welfare services scarcely thought of.)

However, if literacy were not used to encroach upon their preserves, the priests would raise little objection to its adoption and wider dissemination. It would be perfectly possible for people relatively low in the hierarchy of status and power, like the craftsmen of England in the late fourteenth and fifteenth centuries A.D. – when the goldsmiths were forbidden to accept an apprentice 'without he canne writte and Rede' – or the craftsmen of Kerala in the eighteenth century to be encouraged, even put under pressure to learn how to read and perhaps to write for the exigencies of their trades, while the priesthood remained confident of control of its own trade. In North-East Thailand a further assurance for the priesthood was that the sacred literature was written in one script, while another was used for administrative and literary matters.

If, then, literacy is adopted or developed merely as a neutral technology, which facilitates or promotes functions which are already allocated between different groups in a society, its effects are likely to be conserving and stabilising.

In other words, it is not likely to be an immediate or powerful stimulus or reinforcement of other stimuli for change. We may hazard the view indeed, that when literacy is developed wholly within a society and is not imported or adopted from another society, the likelihood is greater that it will indeed help perpetuate existing patterns of relationships between social groups. Unlike, say, the introduction of technologies of mass production, literacy does not necessarily bring about striking changes in the organisation of capital and labour, in the volume of goods, or in the distribution of income and consumption. Neither does it by itself provoke questions and challenges to the established order.

However isolated and conservative a society may be, it is probably never completely static. There will always be individuals and small groups who are seeking better ways of doing things and perhaps better ways of explaining what they observe around them. These generalisations would of course be truer of large societies with external connections, and relatively secure of their survival, than they would of smaller tribal groups cut off from external contact and barely eking out a subsistence. Whether the innovating efforts flourish, are noticed and affect their society will depend first very much on how the groups immediately concerned receive them. If a need for improvement is widely felt and an innovation seems to answer the need without entailing disproportionate costs and inconvenience, it will probably be appreciated and adopted. The innovator will be rewarded by the appreciation in itself, by added status within his group and probably by other benefits as well. He will be encouraged or stimulated to do more, while others might be stimulated to improve yet more upon the improvement. On the other hand, if the innovators' fellows believe that they are already living in the best of all possible worlds, not only is the innovation likely to die of neglect, but the innovator himself may well be discouraged and stifled also. Put more abstractly, where immediate social environments are contented, resigned or fearful of risk, they will tend to be inhospitable to change and by that fact will inhibit even its conception. (They may not kill it altogether, for some individuals simply will not be put down. These latter tend to be exceptional and rare.) This will be all the truer, where an innovation springs from a group of low social status and either does not promote or offer the prospect of even disturbing the interests of people with higher social status, especially if the latter, too, believe they are living in the best of all possible worlds.

Indeed, the values of the higher and ruling groups are critical to the sparking or damping of innovation. If they welcome and seek it, it is likely to occur and develop. If they are indifferent or hostile to it, the impulse will naturally be weakened, though not necessarily extinguished. In South India's Kerala, for instance, the importantly placed Nambudiris of the seventeenth and eighteenth centuries gave all their attention to government, law and religion. They apparently despised trade, experimental science and any form of social innovation. Yet under them, physicians who happened to be of low social rank carried on medical experiment and advanced medicine in Kerala to levels equal to those elsewhere in India. If the Nambudiris had instead behaved, say, as Charles II of Britain behaved towards the Royal Society, with encouragement and patronage, their physicians might not simply have equalled the rest of India, they might have attained international stature as well (Goody, 1968).

Ruling groups are, like other groups, not monolithic. While their members may hold many things in common, they also have their differences. Accordingly, it often happens that various factions have different views on how to act about different possibilities. With regard to an innovation or the extension of a technology more widely in the society, one faction may see the benefits far outweighing the risks, while another may take an opposite opinion. In Britain, at the end of the eighteenth century, many members of the ruling classes judged that the nature and impetus of the industrial revolution, with all the social changes it would bring in its train, demanded that schooling and literacy be spread to all social classes. Their views resulted in a bill for universal elementary education being put before Parliament in 1807. It was defeated. Among its opponents was no less a person than the President of the Royal Society. Carlo Cipolla quotes him:

> However specious in theory the project might be of giving education to the labouring classes of the poor, it would in effect be found to be prejudicial to their morals and happiness; it would teach them to despise their lot in life, instead of making them good servant in agriculture, and other laborious employment to which their rank in society had destined them; instead of teaching them subordination, it would render them factious and refractory, as was evident in the manu-facturing countries; it would enable them to read seditious pamphlets, vicious books, and publications against Christianity; it would render them insolent . . .(Cipolla, 1969)

The interest of this particular illustration is that, besides revealing the divisions and narrow self-interest of sections of the ruling classes, it shows too that men who seek truth of one kind, are not always anxious that other men should be enabled to get hold of truths of another kind. Nevertheless, it is important to note that, although some of the upper classes wished to rein in some of the social consequences of the industrial revolution, those same classes taken as a whole supported the general scientific, technological and economic trends of change. While conservative about social function, rank and status, they were open to, indeed they applauded and paid for, intellectual and technological adventure and innovation. At the time, adventure and innovation were proceeding apace. The importance of the support of the dominant social groups for innovation and innovators is clear here.

The opposition to the spread of literacy in England raises the issue of a technology which is no longer naked and attached only to its original uses. Literacy in England in the nineteenth century had accrued round its base uses of aiding memory and communication a complex of cultural connota-tions. More important it now gave access to a host of political

and social ideas which the rulers of England regarded as subversive. It could no longer be trusted merely to help people do
better in their ordinary stations in life. On the contrary, it
could be expected to give them ideas well above their station.
That the English aristocracy were right in this prediction is, of
course, evidenced by the growth of working men's clubs,
where subversive literature was indeed circulated and
discussed, and where counter-propaganda of an improving
kind seemed not to make much headway. In effect, then,
literacy opened out on to a new culture, creating what we now
call culture-shock and challenging people to re-examine what
they had always accepted without question.

It is in situations of such disturbance, perhaps, that the
people of more than usual intellectual curiosity experience the
impulse to reflect and to explore boldly. They are likely to
find that enough of their social peers and superiors are
sympathetic to provide a climate of tolerance, encouragement, exchange and dialogue. In those circumstances, the
thinkers can raise literacy from a tool of simple record and
communication to a basis for intellectual advance.
Conversely, where a widespread alertness has not been
aroused to possibilities of different views and orders of the
world, the potential thinkers will tend to be deprived both of
the stimulus to think anew and of the supporting social
encouragement to do so. Relative stagnation will ensue. That
is, although intense activity might continue in commerce,
industry, fashion, even in literature and the arts, it will tend
to be confined – contentedly for the most part – within the
parameters of the existing order and culture.

However attractive and plausible such a hypothesis might
appear, can we bring any evidence in its support? Such
evidence would have to be chiefly historical, so that we have
to remind ourselves again that the historical records are of
very little help. In the first place, they are sparse, fragmentary
and not immune to controversy. More important, perhaps, is
that history conceived as a serious, deliberate collecting,
sifting and interpreting of facts with some attempt at
objectivity did not come into being until 2,500 years or so

after writing had been invented. The efforts by Herodotus of Halicarnassus and Thucydides of Athens, both Greeks of the fifth century before Christ, to be objective were radically different from, for example, the accounts of the sack of Babylon – a mere century earlier – by the Judaic Bible and by the victor himself, Cyrus of Persia. The Book of Daniel dismisses it in a sentence, as evidence of Daniel's ability to interpret heavenly signs accurately, while the inscriptions of Cyrus, telling of the diversion of the River Euphrates to give access to Babylon, are more taken up with the glory of the king, than with the wider significance of the city's fall. Third, aspects of history, such as the more subtle ramifications of the encounters between civilisations, did not become areas of close interest to historians until very recently indeed; the consequence is that the phenomena around which we are speculating were simply not observed and no evidence was taken. We have to rely, therefore, on indirect clues, on inference and on guesswork, making the best of what does happen to be available.

To a European, the three most obvious possible sources of examples of the stimulating effects of culture-clash are Greece (the city-states of Ionia, the islands of the Aegean and the mainland), Rome and the modern period from the Renaissance through the industrial revolution. Although a span of some 2,500 years separates the beginning of classical Greece from what we think of as the beginnings of the industrial revolution – half the period during which writing has been used by human civilisations – the latter is in a real sense an outgrowth of what was bravest in the first. Classical Greece had its brightest flowering in the sixth, fifth and fourth centuries before Christ. However, its beginnings went back beyond the eighth century and perhaps even to the twelfth century, when the Mycenaean civilisation of the Achaeans – Agamemnon and Helen of Troy – collapsed and disappeared, along with its script and writings. In the next four centuries, the Achaeans were succeeded by the Hellenes, migrants from the north, who gradually settled in the mainland, the islands and along the coasts of Asia Minor. By the eighth century B.C., they were in firm contact and commerce with the civilisations of the south-eastern Mediterranean, notably Egypt and Phoenicia. The Hellenes or Greeks were relatively new to urban settlement and seem not to have elaborated complex systems of government, priesthood or science. Certainly they seem not to have developed a system of writing.

Their encounter with the pomp, architecture, magical sciences and writings of the southern societies must have caused them some astonishment. They might have been so overwhelmed as to have plumped for one or another of these systems, to have swallowed it whole, adapted their own life-style to it, and become what it is now the fashion to call 'culturally dependent'.

On the contrary, although traces of Egyptian influence can be seen in early Hellenic statuary and architecture, the very facts that, on the one side, there were several civilisations and, on the other, that the Greeks themselves were split into several independent smaller societies, seem to have led them to an eclectic approach adapted to their own ways of doing things. As regards literacy, the Greeks preferred the Phoenician alphabet to the Egyptian logosyllabaries. They took over twenty-two consonants – the Phoenicians managed without symbols for vowels – modified them, added signs for vowels, and ended with an alphabet of twenty-four letters.

Thereafter, they developed their own style in almost every sphere. A constellation of factors may help explain this. The Greeks quite consciously regarded themselves as people different from the 'barbarians' – their sense of the word did not connote primitive savagery, but merely relatively inferior separateness from the Greeks. Second, as their institution of the Olympic Games suggests, they were much given to competition and may have been conscious of competition with other civilisations. Third, and not unrelated, they seem to have preferred to organise themselves as small independent city-states rather than as a large, centralised empire on, say, the Egyptian model, although their sense of competition with each other led to much warfare and conquest between themselves. There was no growth, then, of entrenched priestly and bureaucratic castes. Fourth, although they certainly had their rations of kings and usurping tyrants, the Greeks more than most other peoples tended towards democratic forms of government, and thereby implicitly valued thought and judgment by the individual. Literacy seems to have been widespread among their male citizen population also. Fifth, their success in industry and commerce freed many of them from preoccupations of mere subsistence and paved the way for the development of culture. All in all, then, their societies in themselves and in their relations with other cultures seem to have furnished the conditions in which the leading classes could encourage and support intellectual activity and unorthodoxy with an astonishing degree of tolerance. These same conditions would, of course, have enabled the use of literacy as a springboard for the intellect.

While acknowledging all this, one should recall at the same time that, despite these conditions and despite the availability of literacy, Greece took more than three centuries to attain the full brilliance for which its city-states – mainly Athens – are remembered, and maintained its impetus for less than two centuries. My intent in saying this is simply to repeat that no single technology, like literacy, can possibly explain the workings of a society or culture, even though without it a particular pattern of events could not have occurred.

Rome offers something of a contrast to Greece. Its contacts with Greek civilisation came about less from the travels of Romans and more from the migrations of Greeks: a large part of southern Italy had been colonised by the Greeks even before the Romans made themselves a republic with elected officials at the end of the fifth century B.C. Roman writing was in fact an adaptation of the Greek alphabet and had begun some time before the republic was established. In the third century B.C. all the Greeks in Italy came under the control of Rome by means of gradual military conquest and so, in the mid-second century, did those of mainland Greece. Then, if the Roman poet Horace is to be believed, 'Greece, taken captive, took her captor, Rome, captive.' Rome, in a manner of speaking, became the slave of Greek culture and thought. The Latin orators and poets who began to flourish within a century of the capture of Greece owed most of their inspiration to Greece and their works abound with allusions to their Greek predecessors. In a sense, the Romans simply accepted and did not go beyond Greece in intellectual achievement, despite the excitement generated by Greek philosophy, science and art – and despite having reading and writing available. The encounter of cultures was not a springboard to new and different things, but rather to relatively minor elaborations on long-established patterns.

What might explain this? One hypothesis could be that the Romans did not have sufficient intelligence. That would not stand up to even a cursory review of their attainments in law, administration, engineering, architecture or literature. Alternatively, although intelligent, their interest may not have run to the sorts of areas which intrigued the Greeks. Their genius, some might phrase it, was simply different. The Romans were very good at a range of eminently practical day-to-day affairs: government, building roads, cities, aqueducts, drains, heating systems. A quote attributed to Julia Procilla, mother of Agricola, who was governor of Britain for seven years, illustrates their bent of mind: 'No true Roman spends his time day-dreaming. Even noble dreams cannot take the place of practical deeds.' Although they admired the Greeks, imitated them in many practical ways and their rich even sent their sons to be educated in Greece, the Romans did not follow suit in scientific and metaphysical speculation. Perhaps they saw no immediate use in it. This apparent indifference to what we might call intellectual curiosity may be akin to the fact that, unlike the Greeks, the Romans and their Latin brethren were not thrusting explorers and colonisers. Whereas the Greeks traversed the Mediterranean founding cities all over the place, the Romans expanded out of the plain of Latium into the rest of Italy, then across the water south to Carthage and so on, very gradually and generally in response to threats and challenges. Similarly, they developed their technologies in response to practical problems, to things that needed to be done, and did not devote themselves, generally speaking, to theories to explain causes and relationships.

These suggestions are, of course, matters of social values: just why the Romans should have had this attitude is beyond the scope of this book to explain. It is of interest, nevertheless, that what Julia Procilla told her son 200 years after the capture of Greece would have been approved by a long line of people from the Roman upper classes. Were there other values, then, which would have effected the direction of Roman intellectual activity? For one thing, obedience to the family society and state ranked high, at least officially, and so did the notion of the sacredness of authority – even though, like the Greeks, the Romans were not burdened by a powerful and conservative priesthood. The tendency to accept would be approved, the tendency to question discouraged. For another, although the bitter struggles over political power had resulted in a form of elective democracy with a full male franchise, Rome remained clearly stratified socially, with the upper classes ambivalent about democracy and tending always to prefer an oligarchy. While they resisted dictatorship, they were wary also of demagoguery. Shortly after the extension of Roman rule to Greece and Asia Minor, the difficulties of running a large empire through a system of elective offices gave rise to a process which ended in the dictatorship of Julius Caesar and his heirs. The move towards ever more concentrated power and authority, accompanied as it was by cults of the personalities of the Caesars, would probably have sapped any countervailing tendencies to original and controversial thought. (We might recall here that two of the greatest poems of the Latin Language, the *Aeneid* and *Georgics* of Virgil, not to speak of many more minor ones, were written at least in part as propaganda for the position and policies of Caesar Augustus. The pressure for conformity would have been strong, despite Augustus' own efforts to promote learning and culture, and would of course have grown greater as Augustus was succeeded by Tiberius and others even more notorious.) Consequently, literacy could well have been used to produce great literature within the prevailing norms and values, but the dice were loaded against its being extended into more adventurous applications.

The speculation on the differences between what interested Greek thinkers and what interested Romans has a counterpart in a comparison between the civilisations of India and those of China by Kathleen Gough (Goody, 1968). In summary, she suggests that, because the Indian ruling castes were always more interested in the world beyond earthly reality – indeed for them life on earth was scarcely a reality – they did not produce histories, very accurate measures of time, accurate geography or much experiment in physics or chemistry. The Chinese, on the other hand, being very concerned with the here and now, were distinguished geographers and historians and very exact time-keepers. Boths societies enjoyed the use of literacy. The particular applications they gave to it were very much a function of their social values.

To return to the European scene: the Greek period of intellectual and cultural innovation lasted about four centuries, although its most productive years were perhaps the fifth and fourth centuries before Christ. The Romans had a heyday of some five hundred and fifty years, while their high-water mark spanned about two hundred and fifty. Although the emperor Constantine removed his capital from Rome in A.D. 330, to set himself up in Byzantium (Constantinople) instead, it took another 80 years before Rome was sacked by Alaric, and yet another 66 years before the last emperor of Rome was deposed by the barbarian, Odoacer. Graeco-Roman thought, however, continued to guide the Byzantines. They seem to have added little to the corpus of culture they inherited, apart from the Code of Law which the emperor Justinian had compiled in the mid-sixth century – and an extremely complex manual on court etiquette. Their scholars certainly studied the writings of their forebears, for they wrote out many copies, extracts and summaries. But, despite their assiduous use of literacy for intellectual purposes, the Byzantines did not make much intellectual advance during the 1,100 years that Constantinople endured. In other respects the city provided a civilisation to marvel at: the first crusaders of A.D. 1096 found a place of a million inhabitants with the range of amenities expected in metropoles today – within the limits of the available technologies, of course.

The crusaders had, among other motives perhaps, embarked on a mission of the cross and doubtless had thought of Constantinople simply as a necessary stopping place. They did not foresee that they would in fact spark another great encounter between civilisations. The effects of this one were to shape the world of today, 900 years later. The impulses came from two sources, the one commercial, the other intellectual – and from a fusion of the two. The experience of entirely different cultures – the Byzantine and the Turkish – with different goods and manufactures to offer and willing to acquire what the Europeans might have to offer in return, revealed such opportunities of trade that within two hundred years or so, Europe was trading with India, China and what is now Indonesia. Venice and other Italian and European states, which commanded much of the commerce, grew wealthy, powerful and able to undertake the support of many forms of art and intellectual activity – ways of spending money which might have been prompted by the old Roman patrons. For simultaneously began the rediscovery of Greek and Roman writings, thought, sciences and art – for so long simply stored at Constantinople – which, gestating through a period of 200 years, led to what is conventionally called the Renaissance of the fourteenth and fifteenth centuries. Part of the intellectual heritage gave added impetus to the drive for commerce: the rediscovered work of the geographer Ptolemy, who had lived in the first century A.D., suggested that other trade routes to the East might well lie to the west and south, by sea rather than the caravan ways. The commercial rewards which the discoverers of such routes might gather provided the incentive for a new wave of world exploration. As is well known, not only were new routes uncovered, but a new world as well with – for the Europeans – new civilisations, new goods, new wealth. More importantly, there came a new understanding of the globe. The Europeans were being gradually accustomed to the collapse of long-established beliefs and to the possibility of whole new perspectives. The psychological impact of this must be seen in the context of a cultural background in which a religious authority behaved as though it had the final say on all aspects of truth, and in which established beliefs on many essentially non-religious topics were thought to have been divinely revealed.

In the eleventh century, Europe was Christian, under the spiritual leadership and authority of the Pope in Rome (the great schism between the patriarchs of the eastern and western churches did not occur until 1094, ironically only a year before the first crusade was summoned). The clergy of the church were privileged and powerful in all the states of Europe. They also had close to the monopoly of education and literacy. Some 150 years after the crusaders had 'discovered' Constantinople, Thomas Aquinas was hard at work 'Christianising' the works of Aristotle. What this signifies is that the Roman Catholic church, though authoritarian and insistent – some might say murderously – on its prerogative to protect the truth of Christ, was nevertheless open to the possibility that the writings of the ancients might have relevance to Christian teaching. While the general laity may have been strongly discouraged from theological and other speculation, the clergy and tiny educated classes were given some, if careful, licence for it. Indeed, it is to be noted that the seeds of the Reformation – almost contemporary with the Renaissance – were sown and the movement itself led by priests of the church – John Wycliffe, John Hus, Martin Luther. Similarly, Roger Bacon, a monk contemporary with Aquinas, although beset in his scientific and mechanical speculations by his nervous superiors, was nevertheless protected and encouraged by two Popes. The ambivalence within the church over the limits to be allowed to the new learning was sufficiently strong, on the one hand, to restrain the conservatives from prohibiting it, and, on the other, to give the progressives room to encourage it.

Simultaneous popular discontent with the ways the authority and influence of the church were being abused and recurrent conflicts over powers and jurisdictions between church and secular authorities provided further soil for the growth of another strand of independent thought, that of protest, Protestant thinking and stress on the individual as opposed to the institution. Gradually, the right of the individual to search, to think for himself, to delve further into received wisdom was asserted and accepted, with various qualifications. So, too, was the right of the individual to read for himself. The open rebellions of the Reformation against the Roman Catholic church institutionalised these rights in many European states – even though the traditions of murderous intolerance and authoritarianism were not immediately abandoned. They also confirmed the foundations for individual scientific and empirical research and experiment and paved the way for the English Royal Society, put under royal patronage in 1662. Not only did this institution set out deliberately to foster scientific work, it tried to create also conditions of dialogue, dissemination and cross-fertilisation between scientists. It also established its encouragement through awarding medals and prizes for discoveries and new theories, a tradition of which the modern Nobel Prizes are perhaps the peak.

This open impetus given to thought and innovation led to the industrial revolution, and through it to the techniques among which we live today; so that it can be said that 90 per cent of all scientists known to history are alive now.

What made the difference between the way the Romans received Greek learning and the way the later Europeans did? It is always dangerous to ascribe only one or two causes to processes and events in a civilisation which is at once as variegated and as homogeneous as Europe's. Yet one factor would probably be the Europeans' willingness to read, observe and speculate about things of no obvious immediate value – even to the point, as the famous example goes, of attempting to estimate how many angels could dance on the head of a pin.

A second, more potent, perhaps critical point is the mood of rebellion and assertion against ecclesiastical authority. The Romans had merely accepted what the Greeks had created, perhaps because it added to their civilisation without challenging it radically. In contrast, the Europeans found not only additions, but also apparent challenges. Greek thought could not be accepted just as it came, it needed examination and, very important, it had no authority apart from its intrinsic rationality and appeal. It could be argued with. At the very same time, parts of it could be turned against ecclesiastical authority, to chip away where the church had presumed too far. The confrontation of Greek and Christian civilisations enabled the Europeans to distance themselves from both and to begin carving out new ways of interpreting and using the phenomena of the world.

That literacy and the technologies which have multiplied its media were indispensable to this result is not in doubt. At the very simplest, the Europeans would not have been able to lay hold of the manuscripts to get contact with the ancients, much less study what they had to say. Nevertheless, there seems little doubt that literacy by itself could not explain the extraordinary upsurge and effervescence which, beginning 900 years ago, has vastly accelerated over the past two centuries and shows no signs of exhaustion yet.

A question which is not truly a concern of this book, but which follows naturally, is this: if the Greeks lost their impetus in intellectual development, will the Europeans and kindred western civilisations follow suit eventually? An answer to the question requires naturally that we determine why the Greeks did not ceaselessly build achievement upon achievement down to the present day. Their political and social institutions appear to have been open to temporary innovation; subjugations to successive conquerors did not profoundly interfere with their philosophy and science; their later masters, the Romans, seemed willing to be dazzled by intellectual brilliance – even if they did not go in for it much themselves; they were highly skilled in literacy for all purposes, arithmetic, geometry, philosophy, many sciences; they produced explorers, geographers, historians; they were excellent at argument and debate. Why then did they peter out?

While it would be presumptuous to attempt a complete answer, a suggestion of some of the contributing factors will be in order. Four are proposed here: an excessive respect for tradition, an orientation to the past, complacency and an excessive reliance on the oral mode of teaching.

Their literature provides evidence enough that the Greeks did indeed respect their forebears and traditions and were proud of them. Aristophanes, a writer of comedies in the late fifth century B.C., recalls in various of his plays the valour and values of the men who had fought seventy and eighty years previously at Marathon, Salamis and Plataea. He also attacks with lampoons the new learning espoused by Socrates and the Sophists. Socrates, indeed, was done to death by his fellow citizens, precisely because his questioning was thought to undermine the traditions and morals of the state and to corrupt the young. Past achievements were to be reversed and invoked as guides to present conduct. Reverence and respect for tradition are natural and proper. However, where they loom so powerfully as to confine attention to the achievements and to obscure the limitations, they become both a betrayal and a trap. The betrayal is the usual one of masters by disciples, the letters of the master become more important than his spirit. His discoveries and insights are allowed perversely to choke off further enquiry. And in that lies the trap, for without further enquiry, ossification sets in. The interpreters of the master take on the role of a priesthood to preserve rather than to develop the word. People like Socrates, Plato and Aristotle, once heretics and derided, if not persecuted, become authorities in a pantheon, whose words become dogma; rather than researchers, whose observations, logic and conclusions can be queried, checked, refined and even rejected. The emphasis shifts from research and thought to reading and learning by rote. Advance is thereby precluded and can be resumed only when respect for predecessors is duly leavened by an appreciation of their limitations.

With this reverence grew up habits of measuring intellectual achievement by the volume learned and signalling the acquisition by allusions and quotations. Neither of these habits is uncommon today. Although the almost universal spread of schooling has reduced their fashion somewhat, they are still enjoined upon doctoral students and writers of learned treatises. The difference between the later Greeks' practice of these habits and ours is small, but crucial. Nowadays the parade of learning is intended as a prelude to an original and distinctive contribution, the very originality of which is evidenced by its absence in the array of literature adduced. The critical value is originality or, at the very least, some well-substantiated newness. It is that for which the degree is awarded, and which wins the accompanying prestige. With the later Greeks, the chief achievement was simply knowledge of what the masters had said and the ability to rehearse it.

The tendency to over-value predecessors and, as it were, to freeze in their patterns, may have been bound up with Greek views on the past. They looked back to a Golden Age of heroes and harmony, which may have disposed them to regard the present and future as further departures from perfection and hence all the more to value what their forebears had been able to achieve. Any impulse to break away radically or to launch further from what had been handed down might then have tended to be muted, if indeed it had occurred at all. Among the Europeans, by contrast, one of the results of the Renaissance, the growth of the sciences and the succession of technological revolutions has been the virtual abandonment of the Judaeo-Christian Garden of Eden and the adoption instead of the idea of the perfectability of man, the march *towards* Utopia, not a fall away from it. 'The good old days' no longer have much appeal. 'You have never had it so good', and expectations of uninterruptedly rising standards of living have replaced them.

A rather different, but perhaps more telling, symptom of the change of orientation is the growth of a relatively new genre of literature – science fiction. Trying to imagine what the future is going to be like – and actually making a living from it – is a bright new craft, just over a century old. As far as we know, it is absent entirely from the literatures of all preceding civilisations. It is of course true that Roger Bacon in the thirteenth century A.D. and Leonardo da Vinci in the sixteenth did show astounding prescience about what might be possible. Nevertheless, it was only in 1870 that Jules Verne published his *20,000 Leagues Under the Sea*, which led on through H. G. Wells and others to the current floodtide of fictional life in the future. That people can write books and make films for mass circulation on a global scale, suggests that there has indeed been a radical reorientation of perspective, where nostalgia for lost mansions has been replaced by an almost feverish and insatiable eagerness to realise transformed futures. Literacy is of course a major medium for the spread of the contagion.

Admiration and pride in predecessors may have been coupled with a vivid consciousness that the Hellenic civilisation in virtually all its aspects was one of the most advanced, possibly the most advanced, in the known world. The product would have been complacency – especially as no other civilisation posed an intellectual challenge to the Greek. The corollary would have been the sapping of any spur or incentive to do better or to quest further. Complacency among the Europeans, common enough, has so far been counterbalanced by a variety of forces, some already mentioned, and others which include commercial, military, imperial and technological rivalry as well as what has recently been called 'Disastermania'. Significant groups of people have been disturbed by the actual and potential ill-effects of certain forms of innovation and have agitated for and secured not merely regulation, but innovative counteraction and new research into how benefits can be preserved without undue penalties. The dialectic between 'progress' and 'conservation' is part of the continuing disturbance against complacency. So, too, is the growing alarm about the limits to certain resources now in wide and important use, such as oil and some minerals. Perhaps even more basic is the recognition that the road to truth is strewn with the wreckage of theories: Einstein is both sage and Aunt Sally, but not sacred.

A fourth factor suggested as contributing to the ossification of Hellenic thought, is their manner of teaching. Although the Greeks had writing and books, they did not – if Plato and Socrates are representative of them – much approve of them as aids to learning. Plato is quite explicit about the matter. No book can replace learning through personal instruction, dialogue and discussion. Further, of course, books were decidedly expensive and none too plentiful. Not surprisingly, then, in the schools and academies instruction was mainly oral. Now such instruction is not inherently or necessarily authoritarian. Socrates saw it as the most effective way of stimulating and guiding a student to think for himself and to realise fully the knowledge which lay within him. Many of the best universities of the modern world have used it as part of their repertoire to develop notable thinkers and researchers. On the other hand, the bias towards merely handing out instruction and insisting on the authority of the teacher is always strong and tempting. A climate of reverence for the past and complacency about the present would perhaps ease teachers towards a comfortable didactic rather than strenuous enquiring stance. They would either fail to spark a spirit of search and experiment or, if the spirit sparked spontaneously, tend to snuff it out from sheer lack of interest and disdain.

European and Western teaching and learning, especially in the stages beyond the schooling of children, are much less reliant on person-to-person communications and much more insistent on study through independent reading, observation and experiment. Literacy is a deliberate and required instrument of instruction, reflection, and independent and divergent expression. In this, too, the Europeans clearly diverge from the Greeks.

To the extent that the four factors discussed did in truth contribute to the slackening of the Hellenic intellectual momentum and to the extent that they are not as yet shared by European civilisation, to that extent does European civilisation avoid its own loss of momentum.

Let us now resume the main discussion of the role of literacy in society. If we agree:

that literacy is simply a technology invented for certain practical purposes, but applicable to others and having some unexpected effects,

that learning to read and write does enhance the general ability of an individual to learn systematically and with mental and physical co-ordination,

that yet, in itself, literacy does not radically transform the outlook and functioning either of the individual or of his society, since societies and individuals vary strikingly in their uses and neglect of literacy,

that even so, on the other hand, literacy is necessary to the efficient functioning of large states, large cities and social systems which operate large scale commerce and industry,

that literacy is also necessary to the development of logical thought, the sciences, and technologies founded on the sciences, in other words that literacy really is the technology of the intellect,

what conclusions can we draw about literacy as a 'primordial human right', to use Paolo Freire's phrase? (Freire, 1970).

Before venturing any conclusions at all, we need to ask another question or two. One is: is literacy to be deemed an absolute (or primordial) right, or is it contingent? Second, whether it is one or the other, what obligation is there on whom to ensure that no person is denied the right?

Chapter five
A human right to literacy?

If we regard literacy as an absolute right, we are in effect placing it on a par with the rights to life, food, drink, shelter, supportive social relationships within and beyond the family, personal security and all that is necessary to a physically and psychologically healthy human life – irrespective of the kind of society in which a person finds himself. When we recall that many societies have subsisted for many ages without literacy and that illiteracy has been the state of the majority of mankind for most of mankind's history, it seems implausible that literacy should be accorded an unconditional priority.

If, on the other hand, we regard literacy as a right contingent upon the circumstances of a given society, we would be obliged to identify rights which every individual should enjoy, but would not be able to – either wholly or in part – unless he were sufficiently literate. That the word 'should' has entered the discussion, signals that we have entered the area of norms and values. A society which believes – or whose rulers believe and have sufficient support to enforce – that certain social roles are forever reserved for certain social groups and that unequal status between and within groups is natural, might well hold that only those who need literacy to execute their roles efficiently should have the right to literacy. Others could acquire it, if they wish. Or, as we have noted before, the 'lower orders' might deliberately and openly be disallowed access to literacy. A society where a more 'democratic' view prevails would doubtless aver that, in so far as literacy was necessary to everybody to understand and take part in the conduct of society, everybody should be enabled to become literate, even if many afterwards failed to make much use of literacy.

To take a concrete case, in British society, as in most industrialised societies, the need for universal literacy is plain.

The right to literacy is assured through legislation that requires every child to be educated in school for eleven years. The education is paid for in the main by society as a whole (and only in minor part by the child's family). Nobody would claim that eleven years were necessary for the mere attainment of adequate literacy: schooling is more than the acquisition of literacy and the span of eleven years is as much due to sociopolitical and economic factors, as to educational considerations. Even so, a striking proportion of children – some 10 to 15 per cent – do not achieve adequate literacy, so that questions follow about what is meant by 'adequate literacy' and what length of time seems to be necessary to reach it.

'Adequate literacy' is a concept which has caused much vexation. At some stages of history, for instance, it was thought that working men needed only to be able to read, for what would they want to write about? Some countries today class as literate everybody who says that he can read and write. Others require that a person demonstrate ability to sign his name, before being marked as literate. Yet others will accept a person as literate, only if he can fill in his own census form. In 1948, 'the ability to read and write a simple message' was proposed as a working definition by the United Nations Population Commission. The ensuing discussion led to the notion of 'functional literacy', a level of skill in reading and writing related to needs actually occurring in a country. William Gray formulated it thus in 1956: 'A person is functionally literate when he has acquired the knowledge and skills in reading and writing which enable him to engage effectively in all those activities in which literacy is normally assumed in his culture or group' (Gray, 1956).

The importance of Gray's formulation is the implicit recognition:

that literacy is not a magical or mystic art, but rather a technology for use and application by common people (even though Gray does not assume a 'democratic' polity);

that literacy is chiefly a social skill in the sense that it is mostly used in relations between people and between institutions, so that use and application depend to a major extent on social circumstances;

that this dependence entails the impossibility of an absolute, world-wide standard for attainment; desired attainments are rather to be calibrated against ascertained, actual necessities;

that because 'adequate literacy' depends on social circumstance and because societies change, there needs to be provision to monitor whether standards of literacy are keeping pace with demands on literacy – for example, can a person with x years of schooling understand the income tax return the government wants filled in by every adult citizen?

that a statement of the minimal need of the common person for literacy does not preclude uncommon people from pursuing greater competence and wider uses for their own purposes.

But Gray omitted the dimension of intellectual growth, which the acquisition of literacy might enable. Six years later, in 1962, a group of authorities assembled by UNESCO took Gray's definition two steps further. They added not only the potential for growth, but also the hint that literacy was inseparable from its context of knowledge and application.

A person is literate when he has acquired the essential knowledge and skills which enable him to engage in all those activities in which literacy is required for effective functioning in his group and community, and whose attainments in reading, writing and arithmetic make it possible for him to continue to use these skills towards his own and the community's development.

Gray had said, 'knowledge and skills in reading and writing'. The UNESCO group, by contrast, phrased their formulation to imply that the 'knowledge and skills in reading and writing' were only a subset of the knowledge and skills needed to engage in 'all those activities'. That is, literacy without the rest of the set would be meaningless. Knowledge and skill are as much necessary media of literacy as literacy is a medium of knowledge and skill. An extented implication is that attempting to teach literacy unconnected with the other knowledge and skills required for a set of activities might be a largely futile endeavour. Although it dropped the word 'functional', the formulation reflected the movement towards programmes which attempted to integrate literacy with other instruction in agriculture, arts, crafts, industry and civics or politics.

On the potential for growth, the UNESCO group were ambiguous. By using the phrase 'attainments . . . *make it possible* . . .' the group apparently acknowledged that offering the horse water will not make it drink, that many who attain literacy will not put their skills to more than minimal necessary use. On the other hand, how could it be ascertained whether the point of possibility were reached, unless the new literate actually exploited the possibility? The argument seemed to indicate that if we took two persons who had attained the same level of literacy, one of whom improved his skills and thinking, while the other did not, the first would be literate, but the second not. Perhaps, since they were deliberating in the days when the theory of the 'take-off into economic growth' was gaining currency, they might have supposed that, irrespective of person, a certain threshold of literacy would precipitate self-perpetuating development.

There seem to have been no significant advances on the 1962 formulation. The upshot is that 'adequate literacy' remains the responsibility of a given society to define for itself. The United States of America may, for example, stipulate that a person cannot be regarded as functionally literate unless he can fill in his own annual return of income to the Internal Revenue Service. Cuba, on the other hand, was content in 1961 to deem a person literate if at the end of the literacy course he could write a letter of thanks to President Castro.

(A passing note: it is astonishing that almost 5,000 years should pass between the invention of literacy and serious world-wide attempts to determine how much of it could be regarded as a minimal satisfaction of the – also new – universal human right to it. The fact underlines how recent concern for universal literacy is and, conversely, how normal illiteracy was for most of mankind.)

If 'adequate literacy' can be given no universal definition, it would follow that the time needed to acquire it would similarly be indeterminate and dependent on what was judged to be adequate. However, there is another way of looking at the matter: what degree of skill in literacy ensures that it at least becomes a permanent possession? It is known that reading – still less writing – is not a skill like riding a bicycle, once attained, always retained. The fact is not surprising, if the number of faculties to be co-ordinated is taken into account. However, there does seem to be a threshold of skill, beyond which literacy appears to stick. Because schooling is the major medium through which literacy is taught, it is attractive to measure levels of literacy with completed years of primary school. It has its drawbacks, as will become clear in a little while, but is convenient.

A study done near Bombay in India in 1944–5 by D. R. Gadgil (Gadgil, 1955) suggested that young men with four years of the kind of primary schooling then available in the Satara District seemed to maintain their literacy skills, even though they reported reading little and writing even less. Young men with less than that amount, on the other hand, appeared prone to lapse into illiteracy. In the same general period, 1944–5, the recently founded UNESCO was formulating the universal right to education and recommended that every child should experience at least four years of schooling. Four years then became an accepted minimum and for some years remained the basic block for primary school in a number of countries – but always on the understanding that it was only a minimum, which would be extended as resources demand and, most importantly, policy allowed.

For example, in what is now Zambia, primary schooling was, up until the middle 1960s, divided into three sections. The first four years, Lower Primary, comprised Sub-standards A and B and Standards 1 and 2. Then came Middle Primary of two years with Standards 3 and 4 and finally

Upper Primary with Standards 5 and 6 – eight years in all. A district with a population of, say, 50,000 people might have some thirty Lower Primary Schools, but fewer than ten Middle Primary and possibly only two or three Upper Primary ones. In effect, the then colonial government expected everybody who enrolled in Sub A to continue through to Standard 2 in four years, but certainly did not provide for even half the pupils to go on to Middle Primary, still less to Upper. With basic literacy presumed to have been satisfactorily and permanently achieved, most pupils were considered to have had enough education to be going on with.

The trouble with such a norm is that it must assume that the quality of schooling is more or less uniform both within a single country and, more important, between countries. As has been made clear in research covering twenty-two countries (a twenty-third was added later), this is simply not the case (IEA, 1973). Indeed, one of the leaders of the project gave it as his impression that schooling in some countries achieved in two years what required six years of effort elsewhere. Accordingly, while four years of schooling in some schools of some countries might enable most students to become adequately and permanently literate, the same dose elsewhere might result simply in relapses into illiteracy.

There must also be an assumption that all forms of literacy can be learned in roughly the same amount of time. However, the earlier discussion on logosyllabic and alphabetic scripts would suggest that the latter would need rather fewer years to master than the former. Since those who framed the UNESCO declaration were almost all brought up in the Latin or Greek alphabetic scripts, they may have overlooked the difficulties of Chinese and similar scripts.

Another problem is that, among younger schoolchildren, progress in literacy is partly a matter of maturation. Reading, generally the first skill which children learn, requires the co-ordination of perception, discrimination, cognition, language and memory. These faculties are of course not ready-made, or fully formed, when a child is born. They develop and mature with age. What is more, there are differences between children both in the rate and extent of such development. Some children are ready to undertake reading at an earlier or later age than most, some children learn faster or slower than most. Consequently, setting a limited span of years within a fixed span of ages is hazardous. Treating the four years mentioned by UNESCO as simply a minimum to be progressively increased is obviously essential. Indeed, most governments now try to provide at least six years of schooling for those of their children who can be offered schooling, although one or two have so far confined themselves to five.

Where adults are concerned, using a norm like the equivalent of four or six years of schooling suggests that, if an adult attains the skills attained by the average child in the fourth grade of primary school, he should be permanently literate. Further, if acquiring literacy is partly a matter of maturation, it would follow that adults, being presumably fully developed, should be able to learn faster than children and so reach the fourth grade of skill quicker. This second point has been ascertained both informally in most adult literacy programmes and systematically by the Work Oriented Literacy Projects assisted by UNESCO in Iran and Tanzania. Adults can in a much shortened period of instruction attain equivalences in literacy of three or four years of schooling. What remains uncertain is the matter of retention or permanence. It has not been much studied. What research there is has been hampered by not really knowing what level has been reached in special literacy instruction beforehand. Its findings suggest that there is considerable deterioration in skills, often complete loss, after instruction ends. The losses are consistently higher in rural areas than in towns. Why this should be so is not difficult to imagine.

Two of the usual requisites for the retention of what has been learned are reinforcement and application (an extension of reinforcement). There are grounds for doubting whether graduates of adult literacy programmes easily enjoy either of these conditions. Reinforcement calls for reminders, revisions, stimuli to recall what has been learned and expanding or building on it. Schoolchildren tend – or ought –

to receive all this as a matter of course during a normal school day. Adults in largely illiterate communities will be denied it by the very nature of their lives, which make no use of literacy whatsoever. Those in highly literate communities, on the other hand, will have a greater probability of reinforcement but still only a casual probability. Similarly with the need for application or practice. Societies with high rates of illiteracy tend to be short of reading matter, especially in rural areas and small centres remote from large cities. There is little on which to practise reading, just as the style of life will offer few opportunities to practise writing. Again the difficulties will be less in more literate societies, especially where daily newspapers and other forms of relatively cheap mass literature are available. A more important difficulty, however, lies in the actual level of literacy itself.

The adults generally have been helped to acquire the skills which a fourth- or sixth-grade child of between ten and fourteen years is expected to attain. However, much of the literature a society produces is written by people with skills well above those levels for people like themselves. That is, the skills for 'permanent' literacy may not be sufficient for 'everyday' literacy. It is true that many mass-circulation newspapers do try to write for a grade 6 or 7 level or even more simply than that, while the photo-novella is scarcely a tax on literacy at all. It is also true that by reading matter slightly above the level he has attained, a person can in fact advance his skills. Even so, unless opportunities for such practice are deliberately fostered and arranged – as in Thailand, for example, where newspapers paid for by the government are posted up in some villages – it is probable that the effort involved will be undertaken only by a minority of new literates. The majority, even though their skills be 'permanent', may apply them only a little, advance them not at all and in sum draw almost no use from them. (This will be equally true of young people who leave school with only fourth- or fifth-grade skills in literacy.)

A relevant anecdote may be appropriate here. The Turkish army conscripts every male youth for a period of military service. Because primary schooling is only now approaching universality and still suffers from some premature desertion, a certain proportion of the conscripts are illiterate. They are given a special three-month course in basic literacy with about 400 hours of instruction – much more than is available in most programmes for adult literacy – under specially trained teachers and with a generous array of learning materials and aids. At the end of the instruction about three-quarters of them can read a relatively easy passage, take simple dictation and write a short letter home. In 1972, I asked three of the best graduates to read a short item from a popular Turkish newspaper. Two of them managed well enough, the third had some difficulty. Even so, the best of the three was able to read the item at only thirteen words per minute. This meant that he had had to analyse almost every word before he could read it. He had not reached the point of almost automatic, instantaneous reading. Just how far short of that goal his reading fell, can be gauged from the reading speed of the average adult with ten or eleven years of schooling in Britain – around 200 words per minute. For that young man, despite his success in a 400-hour course, reading was still a labour, even with relatively elementary narrative material. Without further support and reinforcement, he would be apt, not perhaps to forget his skills, but to neglect them.

In sum, the level of literacy which is adequate for the needs of an average citizen has to be determined within the context of a given society. In some societies, it may be well above the level needed for 'permanent' literacy. Similarly, the time needed to make a person adequately literate will vary according to the level determined. However, the period necessary for 'permanent' literacy is likely to be at least four years of schooling for children. In the case of adults, controversy is still vigorous. Some designers of special methods claim excellent results within a few weeks. On the other hand, the evidence available suggests that even 400 hours of instruction are likely to be insufficient for the average adult, unless they are followed up with further stimulus and support.

A final query on this topic: has the development of human societies all round the globe reached such a point that literacy of one level or another must be regarded as an inalienable human right? In the context of societies which have become heavily industrialised, with large urban populations, huge apparatuses of state, industry and commerce, intricately connected with other societies around the world, committed to one extent or another to widespread popular participation in the processes of government – national, local, even international – and hence indissolubly dependent on 'paperwork', on the generation, collection, processing, storage, flow and display of information and ideas, the answer is easily made: yes.

At the opposite pole, there are still some societies or sub-societies where literacy can be useful in only a very tiny, occasional and incidental way in everyday life. Any increase in that use would depend on large changes in the nature and organisation of the society. In such cases, even if the principle of universal literacy were acknowledged, could it be given a high priority for realisation? The response here must take into consideration two factors. One is the extent to which such societies are able to conduct themselves to their own satisfaction without dependence on or intervention from other societies. If they can act without hindrance to maintain and ensure their own welfare and culture, the case for proposing that they make themselves literate cannot be persuasive. Such societies or sub-societies are rare now and comprise relatively few people: hill-tribes in West Irian and Kalimantan (formerly Borneo) come most easily to mind as sub-societies nominally within a larger polity, but virtually unaffected by it.

The second factor to be considered is the degree to which their illiteracy puts them at a disadvantage in their relations with other societies. If it is such as to prevent them from influencing decisions which affect them, or to debar them from reciprocal influence in the affairs of others, or is used – as in bogus treaties with African chieftains in the nineteenth century – to cheat them of their lands or even of their lives –

as has been reported from some South American countries –
then current trends of democratic thought would argue that
such societies or sub-societies should have access at least to
such literacy as would countervail their disadvantages.
(Offering access will not guarantee that the access is utilised,
as many literacy campaigns and records of desertion from
primary schools have demonstrated. Nevertheless, neglect of
a right does not automatically entail its forfeiture. As realisation of the disadvantages of illiteracy – if not of the uses of
literacy – grows, so too will the demand that the right be
available.)

Pooling these two polar types of society and making from
them the human race as a whole, we can note that all but a
very tiny fraction of the human race are now organised into
nation-states. Some of these are very large, embracing
hundreds of millions of people, others are in the very earliest
throes of attempting to fuse into larger units. All of them are
members of the United Nations Organisation and have,
despite a perplexing and paradoxical range of expressions,
accepted the principle of representative democracy in government. These states are growing, by both intent and the force
of circumstances, more complex and more closely integrated.
Few of the currently 'marginal' groups will be able to avoid
incorporation. In these states, by law and regulation, only
those who are literate have access to and control over the
machineries of government, arrange the laws, taxes and
apportionments of resources. Only those who are literate can
buy, direct or at any rate work with the range of technologies
which are changing the wealth, organisation and operation of
their societies; and which will sooner or later pervasively
affect the currently non-literate groups. If these latter are not
to lose out politically and economically, they will have to
acquire the necessary skills of literacy. In short, the need for
literacy already implicates a majority of the human race. If
current trends persist, it will touch virtually the whole of the
race by the end of this century or the early years of the next.
For practical purposes, then, a human right to literacy cannot
but be recognised. What remains at issue is simply when and

how special efforts have to be put in hand to make it easily accessible in particular regions and communities.

The discussion of the right to literacy would be academic, were it not for the fact that universal literacy of fairly high levels is now a feasible proposition. It has been such, let us recall, for less than two centuries in the five millennia during which literacy has been part of the technology of the human race. The cause of this relatively new possibility has been the development of technologies ancillary to literacy, stimulated by developments in technologies possibly unconnected with literacy but leading to such changes in society as have made universal literacy essential to all but a few societies. This observation is related to a more general point: societies tend to be so organised that changes in one mode of organisation or in one technology will impinge, possibly unexpectedly, often indirectly, on other areas of society. The point will be borne in mind as the ancillary or supporting technologies of literacy are examined.

The process of communication through literacy has six steps, each of which calls for one or more enabling technologies. We shall walk through them in an operational sequence, identifying how they are applied and what their social and economic repercussions might be.

Formulation

Before the symbols of literacy can be brought into play, he who wants to communicate something must first formulate it. The better the formulation, the more likely the message is to be communicated in accordance with the communicator's intent. The difficulties of communicating well are most acutely appreciated by those who write for a living, but people can have problems even in formulating a friendly letter (unless of course they simply employ a set of standard phrases, as children often do when scribbling letters home to their parents). It is not surprising then that wherever literacy has been in wide use approaches and techniques have been developed to help people organise their thoughts and words into deeds of good writing. The modern schools of writing and journalism are only the latest successors of people like the Greek, Aristotle, or the Roman, Quintilian, who in the fourth century before and the first century after Christ were laying down the elements of good style in writing and oratory.

They illustrate the tendency for important technologies to generate not only practitioners, but also teachers and improvers. In other words, employment is created at one remove from the technology itself, and along with it an additional profession. This implies an additional social interest group, which might organise itself to gain official recognition, to control access to the profession and to regulate remuneration. However, because the formulation of words is still a personal and internal process, not yet replaceable by machines – even though often shared by committees – the technologies of formulation remain in the realm of general mental discipline, and sundry advice and tips on how to do it. It does not ramify into sophisticated materials and machinery and hence into a congeries of arts and skills not ordinarily associated with literacy.

Inscription

The case is rather different with the second step, inscribing. Here the operation demands at least two articles, the material on which the script is to be marked and the instrument with which the marking will be done. The very early means, clay tablets and sharpened sticks, would probably not have had much impact on social organisation, apart from perhaps creating employment for the bakers of clay tablets. However, their limitations of clumsiness, messiness, weight, volume (from the view of storage) but small size (such a medium could scarcely cope with books and newspapers) must have paved the way for something better. They would have irritated and stimulated some people into pondering how to get the job done more efficiently. The subsequent development, perhaps as early as 3000 B.C., of writing material from the papyrus reed would have gone a long way to answering their dissatisfaction: indeed, papyrus did not fall into disuse until about the fourth century A.D.

Papyrus itself illustrates how a resource and its associated technologies, exploited for one set of purposes, can be turned to unexpected uses. The reed was found by the Egyptians to be valuable and versatile. Its pith could be used as an emergency, low-grade food. The more slender of its stalks were woven into baskets, the thicker into light boats for transport on the Nile. Its fibres were transformed into string and rope, sails, awning, tents and mats. Its roots were both a consumer good in the form of fuel and durable goods in the shapes of household utensils. On top of all this, someone or some group of persons worked out – perhaps from the fact that sails could be painted – that, if the fibres were laid in cross-wise layers no more than two or three deep, were then dried, compressed heavily and finally smoothed, they formed a good surface for writing. But of course this surface could not be scratched as clay tablets were. Marks would have to be laid or painted on it. That is, a paint or an ink would be needed and so too would either a brush or some instrument which could both hold the ink and transfer it controllably to the writing surface. One technology thus demanded another, and the use of one reed led to the enlistment of others. These had thin, hollow stems, which could be split, sharpened and employed much as 'dip' and fountain pens are today. Correspondingly, suitable inks were developed from the paints already known to the Egyptians and others. The earliest were possibly mixtures of finely ground charcoal and thin glue: the Chinese of around 2000 B.C. even had a waterproof ink made from lamp-black. Later, the Romans used sepia from cuttle-fish.

All three items, 'paper', reed-pens and inks, would have generated employment and income for producers of raw materials, processers and traders. They would have been part of the social organisation of production and exchange. However, the numbers of such people would have been relatively small, if only because the literate groups of businessmen, administrators and priests whom they served were themselves such tiny minorities. Also, probably only the producers of 'paper' would have needed to engage full-time in their service to literacy: the pen and ink producers and traders would probably have been in the business only as a side-line to supplement other sources of livelihood – as was the case with the producers of papyrus reed, which, because of its diverse uses, was turned by the Egyptians into a plantation crop. The fact that manufacturing papyrus 'paper' was a laborious, time-consuming and hence expensive process was part of the explanation for the restriction of literacy to small groups of rich and influential people. The monopoly of political power and the limited scope for actually using literacy would certainly also have been major contributors to this restriction. Nevertheless, it is arguable that, if the technology of papyrus 'paper' production had been cheaper, so that the supply could have been more plentiful and more easily accessible, the demand for and promotion of literacy would have been correspondingly greater. On the other hand, it has still to be borne in mind that as the example of inventions in China will testify, political and social considerations are entirely capable of overriding technological possibilities.

Other writing materials, like bamboo, bone, silk and parchment, shared with papyrus 'paper' this feature of restrictive expense. The possibility of significantly cheapening the process first occurred in the very early second century A.D., when a Chinese minister, T'sai Lun, is said to have worked out how to make paper from boiled and pulped vegetable fibres. Whatever the effects in China, it took six hundred years for the secrets of this new invention to percolate thence, by way of prisoners of war, to southern Russia. The fact perhaps illustrates how jealously human groups can guard their property and interests. A further four hundred years passed before the Arabs introduced paper-making into southern Europe in the twelfth century and not until yet another three hundred years had elapsed, could paper be said to have superseded parchment – which had superseded papyrus in Europe round the fourth century A.D. Nowadays, the advent of powered machinery coupled with energetic research into a variety of materials convertible into paper has made it possible to churn out the commodity at rates of close to 1,000 metres per minute in a staggering range of qualities. The volume of newspapers, magazines, journals, books, writing pads – to mention only those articles connected with literacy – which is produced daily around the world is ready evidence that paper has indeed become cheap and abundant.

Even so, paper by itself would not make universal literacy possible. The coming of paper brought a change of pen, for the writing surface was smoother and required a finer point. The answer this time, around A.D. 500, came not from water plants, but from water birds: the quill feathers of swans and geese were found, when sharpened to a point, to provide the convenient combination of reservoir and flow for scribes. In its turn, the quill pen stimulated the development of the pen-knife, which could be easily and safely carried on a writer's person, and remained in use almost to the end of the eighteenth century A.D. However elegant the pen, so long as it remained the sole means of inscribing on paper, it too constituted a limitation on the spread of literacy. For, in current parlance, it is a highly labour-intensive technology. So long as it needed one person to wield one pen to write down only one word at a time, any scope for wider literacy that cheap paper offered was narrowed by the expense of multiplication or reproduction (this observation would remain true, even if the electric typewriter had replaced the pen, without any change occurring in the technology of reproduction).

It can of course be contended that having supplies of cheaper paper actually did by itself make wider, perhaps universal, literacy possible, simply because it enabled everybody to indulge in at least private correspondence and record-keeping. Although such a view is possible in principle, it has two weaknesses in practice. One is that reading is the more important skill of literacy, the second that writing is the more difficult to master. Both have implications for the application of and hence the motivation to learn literacy. Although in historical sequence, writing necessarily preceded reading – the code had to be invented before decoding could occur – the latter is much more widely practised. The reasons are simply that reading enables people to get hold of news, information, ideas, entertainment; whereas writing only enables people to give out such commodities. Getting matter is not only a much easier business, it also makes much more obvious sense and appeal. Most people are readier to acknowledge that they need information, than that they have much to offer others, even though they might like to pen the occasional letter. As was observed earlier, those who want to communicate prolifically and widely in writing are generally a very small minority. If there is not much to be read, so that reading cannot offer access to what people feel is worth knowing or enjoying, the motivation to learn reading is destroyed. If persuading people to read were hard, persuading them to learn to write would be still harder, if only because it is much more laborious and its uses more obscure. We know from records of as early as the fourteenth and fifteenth centuries in England and elsewhere, that many men could read but not write: that is, although they had the capability to take the extra step, even by themselves, they did not. Their inhibitions may have been many and may have stemmed from many sources, not least their social position and what convention deemed their 'proper place'. Nevertheless, the fact remains that these people were not moved to take up writing, even though they had mastered reading. The argument, in short, is that, for most people, the desire to read is a necessary precondition to the will to write. If there is limited use in reading, because access to reading material is itself limited by expense, by distance, by inconvenience, by sheer scarcity, there will be a correspondingly limited sense of need for reading and an even more limited sense of need for writing. In social terms, both governors and governed would tend to share the pragmatic view that literacy was not an essential item of universal education, but should properly be limited to those whose social functions required it. Few societies would have adopted the view of Paolo Freire that illiteracy is intrinsically a limitation to the human consciousness, personality and development (although our speculations in the last chapter will suggest that Freire is right).

Reproduction

If we accept for the nonce that universal literacy is not feasible without an abundance of reading matter, the importance of the third step, multiplication or reproduction, becomes obvious. For millennia, the pen wielded by a copying scribe was the only way to make several copies of a document. The results in terms of the expense and scarcity of books and other public reading matter can be easily deduced. The possibility of abundance came nearer with the development of paper. It is probably no simple coincidence that the country which first saw paper produced, China, also saw the first steps towards the mass reproduction of documents. The very availability of paper was a stimulus, albeit slow-working, towards a better and more intensive use of it. The Chinese had long known the principle of marking materials with designs and letters carved in relief out of wood. They did not convert it to printing, until some 700 years after the invention of paper: the oldest known printed book dates from the mid-ninth century A.D. (Despite this, literacy did not become widespread in China until the mid-twentieth century, when the Marxist-Leninists took over the government of the country and instituted a radical transformation of the society. The fact recalls the point made earlier that political and social considerations can override technological possibilities. Whatever the difficulties of a logosyllabic script, what the Marxist-Leninists have managed – and what was managed in the nineteenth century by the imperial regimes of Japan – could have been managed by the imperial regimes of China, had they been so inclined.)

In Europe, the first 'block-books' of wood appeared in the mid-fourteenth century, five hundred years after China, but only about two hundred years after paper-making had been introduced. The step from paper to easier multiple reproduction occurred rather more quickly than it had in China. Even so, one more century passed before Johann Gensfleisch von

Gutenberg and his associates in Germany developed movable types and began printing as we know it. Books, pamphlets, posters and other documents could now be reproduced both in larger numbers and much more speedily than before. For another four hundred years, they remained relatively expensive and hence mainly the domain of the well-to-do and scholarly. Nevertheless, the possibility of universal literacy was now real and the needs for it becoming increasingly apparent, as Chapter two noted.

Concomitantly, the technology of literacy was coming to depend on an ever-widening range of other technologies. Even up to Gutenberg, writers and their readers needed the paper-makers, the parchment-makers, the ink-makers, possibly even some pen-makers. Gutenberg may have started his pilot work with wooden type, but he had to call in metalworkers in the persons of the goldsmith, Trust, and his son-in-law, Schoeffer, to bring his ideas to fruition. To these were joined the woodworkers, who had to devise the first printing presses. With the harnessing of mechanical power through steam and then electricity, and the advances of science and technology in the industrial revolution, chemistry, metallurgy, machine engineering, photography, electronics were all extended and applied to the vaster and cheaper multiplication of reading material and hence to the expansion of literacy. The outcome is a breathtaking spectrum of options for reproducing written material. At one end are the gigantic sophistications of the mass-circulation newspapers, gushing with several millions of copies per day, and some with centres for virtually simultaneous reproduction in two or more countries. At the other end are the more restricted but no less striking instant photocopying machines, and their humbler forebears, the stencil duplicators.

(A parenthetical observation: if literacy benefited from the spin-off of technologies developed originally for other purposes, it was not the only beneficiary. The advances in reproduction and printing were boons also to the dissemination of music, especially of orchestral scores, and to the wider enjoyment of paintings and sculpture.)

Storage and distribution

Inscribing and reproduction, accompanied as they have been by rising tides of literature of all kinds, have had to be supported by the fourth and fifth steps of developing capacities to store and retrieve and then to disseminate all the material which has issued for public reading. The point need not be laboured, since evidence of it is everywhere apparent. The gargantuan national and university libraries have had to devise ingeniously neat systems for classifying and locating their materials. Even more, they have had to have recourse to microfilm in order simply to store portions of the stuff – books are no longer handy enough – and to computers to help them keep track of it. Publishing firms have opened outlets wherever a flicker of literacy showed. This is true not only of the capitalist enterprises seeking profit, but also of the missionary undertakings spreading the messages of Christianity, Islam or Marxism.

Correspondingly, where these supports have not developed fast enough, there have been lapses into illiteracy. Indeed, ensuring their presence and efficient operation remains one of the problems of states which are relatively poor and are striving to develop economically and socially.

The evolution of these ancillary technologies provides an illustration of the social repercussions of changes in technology. The steps of inscribing, reproduction, storage, retrieval and distribution now account for significant proportions of employment – in an array of different crafts – and business all over the world, but particularly in the intensely industrialised countries. The people engaged in them are interested in satisfying the various needs for reading and writing material. They may be equally concerned in maintaining the need for their services. Recent disputes between different craft groups, for instance, over the reorganisation of work implied by changes in printing technology have led to the paralysis of famous newspapers. What have been at work simultaneously are two factors, common in human organisations. One is a cycle of reciprocating reinforcement between service to others and service to self, i.e. meeting a demand for reading material and ensuring the continuation of one's job. The second is the interplay of interests, sometimes shared, for example, keeping a newspaper profitable, sometimes in conflict, for example, disputing how the profits should be divided.

Reading

In the last step of the processes of literacy, as in the first, ancillary technologies have had a much less spectacular impact than those of the intermediary steps. The formulator, despite the pen, pencil, typewriter, stenographer, dictaphone or even the computer-as-secretary, is not much helped in the actual process of formulation. He depends almost entirely on his own abilities. Professional writers might devise little disciplines and techniques to suit their own particular personalities and metabolisms, but there are as yet no machines or even drugs to help them organise their thoughts, arguments, descriptions more rapidly, cogently, or plangently. Most rely on native wit, cultivated by hard grind. Similarly, the receiver or reader depends almost entirely on his own faculties – eyes, brain, concentration and intelligence –aided by a modicum of training. (It is true that in the past much reading was done aloud, so that many receivers had only to be attentive listeners. Even so, listeners who could make notes, were of course at an advantage in subsequent discussions or examinations. Even today, in countries where textbooks are neither available nor easily accessible, university students who can take good notes are not only better equipped for their examinations, they are also in a position to earn cash from their less efficient but no less anxious coevals.)

Although readers have in the main to be self-reliant, many of them owe their continued ability to read to the science and technologies of optics. Reading-glasses, bifocals, contact and photosensitive lenses are only the latest part of a long line of technological aids to compensate for genetic defects, diseases, accidental damage and deteriorations of age, which affect the human eye – for which reading and writing are only two of a range of activities: spectacles are useful also to illiterate people. Nevertheless, spectacles constitute the present limit of mechanical help to the reader. Beyond them, effort has had to be confined simply to increasing the understanding of the processes of reading, so that the efficiency of the reader can be improved through various disciplines and the techniques of speed-reading. These include attempting to read soundlessly, by neither uttering the word physically nor allowing the mental equivalent to occur. In short circuiting the sound-values of written words, speed-readers are in fact approximating the process of logosyllabic scripts. Speed-readers also strive to avoid inadvertently reading a phrase or sentence twice or thrice over, to stretch their eye spans, so that they can ingest six or seven words in a single glance, to 'sample' books, so that not all the words need to be read for the main substance of meaning to be extracted. The success of these exercises, as the success of a writer, depends not on machines or drugs, but only on the effort and perseverance of the individual reader.

In sum then, the technologies ancillary to literacy have put the following advantages before the human race:

the possibility of universal literacy

they have enabled one writer to reach a million or more readers within a few hours

conversely, they have enabled one reader to peruse several hundred writers

they permit a writer to reach a correspondent half-way around the world within a few hours by telegram or telex or within a few days by airmail they have driven up the demand for writers and reading matter and hence for craftsmen, paper, ink and large organisations employing large numbers of people.

On the other hand, in the essential acts of communication by literacy, writing the word and reading it, the ancillary technologies subside into the background and give way to the human factors which determine the transaction between two persons, the writer and his reader. To balance this focus on individuals, let us recall that not only the technologies, but the very possibilities (or denials) of transactions by literacy are the outcomes of long processes of political economy in which most known societies have engaged internally and internationally.

Further reading

Paolo Freire (1970), *Pedagogy of the Oppressed*, New York, Herder & Herder.
David Harman (1974), *Community Fundamental Education*, Lexington, D.C. Heath

Chapter six

The costs and the future of literacy?

We have considered literacy as a technology which can be put to a variety of uses by people of a variety of businesses and opinions. We have suggested also that it has proved over the centuries to be more potent than its first inventors had imagined. It enabled the human intellect to maintain complex forms of human communication and organisation and, as an unexpected bonus, to develop new systems of thought, logic, science and technology. At the same time, its potentials have been differentially exploited by different societies and by different groups and individuals within societies. In politics, literacy has been used to perpetuate, even accentuate and deepen, social divisions and inequalities of power, authority and status. Contrarily, it has been a major vehicle for the promotion of democratic and egalitarian modes of government. In some societies, such as those grounded in derivatives of Marxism, an insistence on and enormous effort for universal literacy and schooling have been accompanied by fairly close guidelines on how freely literacy may be utilised, neither indiscriminate access to all literature nor unbridled rein to written expression has been permitted, nor has a diversity of political views. In religion, written texts have been used by conservatives to buttress established beliefs and institutions, and by freer thinkers to undermine or modify them. Some have exercised literacy to mystify their readers – theologians, civil servants and lawyers have often been accused of this sin; others have laboured painfully to make all plain to everyman. In some societies, literacy has been used chiefly to maintain and lightly to embellish the *status quo*. Elsewhere, it has been a major tool for new thinkers, inventors, revolutionaries. Some people may apply their skills of literacy, arduously acquired, merely to read comic books and scribble a line on a holiday postcard. Others may spend most of their working hours reading and writing memoranda and still devote much of their leisure to reading and writing memoranda in other fields. Yet others may deliberately direct their skills of literacy to clarifying and advancing man's understanding of himself and his world. Literacy may not have been available to some people for large parts of their lives; even so, they persevere to make the most of an adult literacy programme. Their very neighbours, in much the same boat as themselves, may in marked contrast decline to make a similar effort. Kathleen Gough sums up the possibilities:

> Literacy is for the most part an enabling rather than a casual factor, making possible the development of complex political structures, syllogistic reasoning, scientific enquiry, linear conceptions of reality, scholarly specialisation, artistic elaboration, and perhaps certain kinds of individualism and alienation. Whether, and to what extent, these will in fact develop depends apparently on concomitant factors of ecology; inter-societal relations, and internal ideological and social structural responses to these. (Goody, 1968)

One word of her summary hints that there might be an unexpected price to pay for the unexpected benefits of literacy. 'Alienation' in the sense used here is an attitude of estrangement, even hostility, on the part of an individual towards his society. He has the feeling that he is no longer at one with his community. How might the possession of the skills of literacy bring this about? To explore this supposition it may be better to start from the extreme case of an illiterate person in a totally illiterate society in contact only with societies similar to itself. From the conditions in which literacy has been developed historically, we can surmise that such societies will be small and relatively simple in their organisations.

An illiterate can get to know things by himself through observation, trial and effort. By definition, he is denied the possibility of learning through studying documents. In the main, most of his knowledge and skill will be acquired in dialogue with second or several parties. In the nature of things, the second party will almost always be from the close family or a group in fairly regular contact with the first and likely to have much in common by way of beliefs, values, habits, livelihood – in short, a common culture. They will tend to support and reinforce each other's world-views – although they may also have much daily detail over which to dispute – and strengthen their common culture. Simultaneously, they will also be restricting it, since they will be likely to offer each other little wider experience or any cultural challenge. Whatever their personal differences, they will be in cultural consonance. Their world would be culturally homogeneous. Change in it would be slow, imperceptible and possibly not realised by those involved. Recall the centuries which elapsed between the advances in the technologies of literacy even in relatively literate societies.

Two important aspects of cultural homogeneity and slow change are the sense of oneness or identity with one's community and the sense of security flowing from the probably unconscious certainty that there is only one way of interpreting society and the world.

A partial contributor to cultural homogeneity is the limitations of memory. These limitations are four. First, there is the actual volume which can be stored and mobilised by either an individual or a collection of individuals, each laying hold of much that is common to all others, plus some part which is particular to himself and to his special sub-group. The sum of such skills and lore in the various crafts, sciences, social and family histories and legends can be far greater than lies within the capacity of one individual to retain, yet is necessarily more finite than can be indefinitely stored on materials more permanent and more indefinitely expandable than the human memory. To observe this is not in the least to belittle the feats of, say, the Doric bards who carried in their heads the tens of thousands of lines of the *Iliad* and *Odyssey*. Yet it is worth recalling at the same time that these two epics were virtually the only two major bodies of oral art to be bequeathed to the later literate generation of Greeks.

Second, the converse of the limitation of volume is the tendency to forget – in two senses. One is losing something entirely from the memory, the other is transmitting something imperfectly. For example, points which are passed on to one set of students at one time may through some distraction be overlooked in the instruction of another. All that is received may not be handed on.

A third limitation is the element of discard or more or less deliberate forgetting. It is necessarily selective, but the criteria for selection are not necessarily fixed or fully thought through. Selection operates on two streams of knowledge. One is what is handed on, the second is what is picked up through actual experience. In trying to augment tradition from current experience, it may be expedient or just convenient to jettison what is already tradition. For example, the oral histories of people without literacy often compress or skip generations in order the more easily to accommodate new history.

Fourth, whether selection is conscious or not, memory will be subject to biases of interest and convenience: what is not compatible with previously held views or is irksome to particular interests will be likely to be suppressed and omitted from the repertoire of tradition. Bias is not a monopoly of illiterate societies, of course. The varying accounts of the Battle of Waterloo by British, French and German history books are sufficient evidence of that; and in his novel *Nineteen Eighty-Four* George Orwell pointed to the possibilities of rewriting histories wholesale every few years or so in order to match sudden changes of state policy. Nevertheless, whereas written accounts can still be compared and verified, biases in oral accounts are less amenable to detection. Selection and bias will tend to ensure that what is remembered and incorporated into tradition harmonises with the world-view and values of the community in question. Cultural homogeneity is maintained thereby.

What these four limitations imply is that the totality of the illiterate culture we have hypothesised is bounded by human memory and is relatively consistent within its own terms. This means that a very large proportion of the society's culture is accessible to the ordinary individual. The culture cannot proliferate beyond all possibility of comprehension, nor does it break up into very disparate streams or coteries, including some members of the society and excluding others. It remains common to all the community and also manageable by all of them.

The polar contrast to this extreme is the modern specialist who, as the saying goes, 'learns more and more about less and less, until he knows everything about nothing'. He is found notably in the rich, industrialised, heavily urbanised, almost universally literate societies of the world, but also among the highly schooled minorities of less literate nations. He finds himself in a situation which has no precedent in history. The current accumulation of knowledge, the momentum of research and development in scores more fields and sub-fields, the pace of producing literature, ephemeral and durable, are such that people are faced with a set of difficult choices. They can know a little about a lot, being either hailed as 'broad humanists' or excoriated as 'dilettantes'. Or they can know a lot about a little, being respected as 'authorities' or despised as 'narrow specialists'. They can strain to work out some compromise between the two poles – and risk being labelled 'mediocrities'. Or, like Candide, they can cop out altogether, content themselves with cultivating their own backyards and resign themselves to nonentity. What nobody can do is pretend to master or keep pace with the growth of all aspects of any of the industrialised cultures. Each person, whatever his capacities must acknowledge ignorance and inadequacy in the *majority* of the fields of knowledge and experience now open to the human race. That is to say, no person can experience the wholeness of his or her culture. He has to be resigned to partiality only.

Further, the partiality occurs in an 'expanding universe' of culture, if we may invoke an astronomical notion for help. Just as points on the surface of a balloon move away from each other, as the balloon swells, so the expansion of the culture of a society moves its members away from each other, at once decreasing the proportion of the culture to which they have access and attenuating what they hold in common. The effects are, on the one hand, to intensify specialisation and on the other to reduce the possibilities of communication between members of the same general culture. The irony arises that a basic technology of communication, literacy, can be the one contributing instrument to situations in which communication is seriously impeded.

Simultaneous with the experience of partiality in given cultures, is the collision of cultures. The complex societies of the world are no longer isolated from each other. They overlap and interpenetrate each other to such depths that despite persisting differences there is inevitable concern over the homogenisation and possible consequent impoverishment of the world's cultures. Never before, for instance, has it been possible for a world-view to achieve global power within less than a century after its originators' deaths, as Marxism has done. The interpenetrations are currently unequal. It is true to say that the rest of the world has been much more influenced by the values, ideas and technology of the North Americans and Europeans than vice versa. Yet, just as the confrontation of Greek thought and mediaeval Christianity contributed to the accelerating ferment of the past 900 years, so the confrontation of the European world-views with those of Asia and Africa, exacerbated by past and continuing confrontations over resources, technology and power, may not only maintain the momentum of cultural interchange, but even reverse its direction. Our present concern, however, is with the effects of the interpretation.

People who strenuously use their literacy can present themselves with a variety of world-views to challenge and compete with their own. They can also review varieties of aesthetic values – visual, literacy, linear, chromatic – and decide which of them to incorporate or reject. In the process, the sense of the uniqueness of their culture and the certainty of its correctness would be modified or evaporate altogether. The options would then be several: a rejection of all challenges, or a complete surrender to and espousal of one of them; a new personal synthesis to take account of what seems valid in other views – generating as many syntheses as there are thoughtful, literate people, a form of extreme individualism or a state of such uncertainty that detachment and alienation from all views ensues.

All this is certainly within the realm of plausibility. To what extent is it already realised and, more to our purpose, to what extent might it be attributed to literacy? Neither question has been empirically tested, so that answers to them must depend on the personal experiences, impressions and speculations of individuals. Perhaps at this point we might remind ourselves that we have been discussing only the extremes of total illiteracy and of isolated specialisation by means of literacy. Between these poles are a variety of forms in the organisation of societies and even more in the responses of individuals. Each form of society is characterised by some degree of specialisation of function among its members. By that fact it is necessarily characterised also by some 'partiality' of participation in culture, for few can specialise in all the specialities available. Some divisions between groups ensue and may well be accompanied by hierarchial distributions of wealth and power. Areas where lack of common ground makes communication difficult follow naturally and so do forms of alienation between groups. A situation then becomes possible where, as it was once epitomised, when one Englishman opens his mouth, another despises him. What give a moral colouring to these phenomena are the degree to which they obtain and their effects on what might be considered 'just social relations' – concepts of which, let us remind ourselves, have varied between societies over the millennia.

Over against the possible ill consequences of specialisation have to be set its benefits, which are again a question of values. The momentum towards increasing specialisation can be explained only by the other side of its coin. Two of its consequences may be divisiveness and isolation. Two others are interdependence and enrichment. People depend on the specialities of each other to have various needs and wants satisfied. Life can offer a great many more amenities – physical, occupational, intellectual, cultural – through the proliferation of specialities than it can where every person must be self-sufficient, working to meet his own needs. Even the 'do-it-yourself' handyman, for instance, judging the benefits of specialisation and interdependence to have grown too costly, can do it himself so readily only because some people specialise in making it easy to meet his whims.

(We can note in parenthesis that interdependence is not an unalloyed gain. It is useful when all those interdependent on each other can be relied on. When reliability is uncertain, interdependence   generates   enhanced   vulnerability. Correspondingly, it entails a distribution of power between all the members of a given net of interdependence. Such distribution is seldom equal, but in proportion to the salience of the needs which a particular group of members meets. One group can accordingly exert more pressure than another – but may, of course, be counterbalanced by other forms of power.)

Specialisation and interdependence are both possible only because people have needs, values and wants in common. We have the double paradox that without a sufficient community of need, specialisation is not feasible, while the more specialised and isolated we become, the more dependent we are on the community for the satisfaction of most of our needs. Carpenters could not subsist unless enough people wanted wooden artefacts. Researchers in evolution, astronomy or archaeology could not continue, unless enough people with enough means valued their findings, whatever their practical outcomes. Reciprocally, carpenters and researchers need farmers, weavers and a host of others to cater to the needs of their wider lives.

Against the possible ills of excessive specialisation, then, have to be weighed
their probable occurrence and their proportion
within a society taken as a whole,
the possibilities of counteracting or mitigating them,

if they do occur,
the benefits forgone and the benefits regained, if the specialisation is reversed.

What estimate can be made of the role of literacy in diversification, specialisation, social divisiveness, 'partiality' of participation, alienation? As one of an array of technologies, literacy can be only one element in these processes. Historically, as we have noted, it has appeared only when diversification has been fairly well advanced and only when a recognisably urban culture has emerged. Literacy cannot, then, be considered an originating force for diversification, specialisation or urbanisation. But it has been an essential lubricant for the further development of specialities which have depended on the accumulation or synthesis of recorded information and on the iterative refinement of hypotheses and conclusions.

Correspondingly, literacy cannot be considered an originating force for social divisiveness. On the other hand, it has been very much the technology of activities which have required much mental effort. It has been of less use to those which have demanded manual strength and dexterity. From this follows the relative neglect of literacy in manual, rural and housebound occupations – a neglect often accentuated, encouraged, even institutionalised by hierarchical divisions between mental and manual occupations. As the ancient Egyptian inscription declared, 'The scribe is released from manual tasks: it is he who commands.' Equally, the universal dissemination of literacy has been pressed by those who have wanted to see a more egalitarian order among men.

As regards 'partiality' of participation in the culture of a society, literacy can be seen as having an influence towards more restricted 'partiality' and also towards more comprehensive participation. On the other hand, it facilitates the accumulation and expansion of knowledge and literature. It thus makes 'partiality' more likely. On the other hand, by providing access to the accumulation in a manner at once independent, easy and relatively rapid – and not available to the illiterate – it enables people to participate more widely than they could without it. Illiteracy in an illiterate or oral culture permits participation in a greater proportion of the culture than even well-developed literacy in a highly literate and extensively diversified society. In terms of absolute grasp, however, literacy offers access to a much more substantial field of experience and thought than does illiteracy.

It is possible that encounters with alien cultures and philosophies may alienate a person from his own, indeed from all. It may also be the case that a surfeit of literacy renders a person peculiarly vulnerable to alienation. However, experiences of several cultures are not the exclusive privilege of the literate. The illiterate can suffer them actually in their own society, if it is one with partial literacy or composed of many nationalities, as were say the Roman and Turkish empires. These possibilities were expanded for those illiterates who travelled in caravans and ships to numerous alien societies in search of trade and other sources of wealth. Most of the men who went with Magellan, da Gama, Columbus, Cabot, Drake in all directions out from Europe would have been illiterate and doubtless much astonished by the civilisations they met along the way. The current experiences of illiterate and little-schooled migrants to the industrialised countries would be similar. The question is whether the literate are likely to be more disoriented by the novelties than the illiterate.

If one thinks in terms of a poor rural illiterate migrant arriving in the capital city of a country which is strange in race, climate, culture, work habits and technology, the presumption that he would likely be disoriented and possibly alienated from his culture would be strong. There could be an alternative hypothesis, however: the very impact of the strangeness might alienate him from the new culture and make him take even more tenacious refuge in his own – at least temporarily. If, for contrast, one thinks in terms of a scarcely literate British sailor in the late eighteenth century, voyaging round the ports of the world, conscious and confident of the power and superiority of British culture, the presumption is more likely to be that the strange cultures he met would have affected him only in a tangential and superficial way. Indeed, he would most probably have been confirmed in his prejudices, not shaken.

Similarly, the 'brain-drain' of highly, even exceptionally literate people from the poorer countries to the richer suggests that many tend to adopt at least some of the habits, customs and modes of thought of their new work-places, while simultaneously trying to maintain much of their own culture. They may in consequence be subject to stress and alienation from both cultures. By contrast, the engineers, doctors, educators, managers, missionaries and volunteers – all highly literate, also – who go from the richer countries to work in the poorer, appear much less prone to adapt to local environments and customs. On the contrary, they are more often accused of forming 'expatriate ghettoes' or colonies, in which they persist in their own ways. Even worse, they are widely suspected of being loftily critical of their host societies. When they do take notice of its culture and thought, it is likely to be as tourists, rather than as serious students. Their experiences, like those of the sailor, would more likely be tangential.

Serious students, on the other hand, may present a different case. Yet with them a sense of proportion needs to be retained. An illiterate person in today's world is so extremely unlikely to be a student of comparative philosophy, religion, politics or sociology, that the contingency can be left out of account. Even among the literates only very, very few devote themselves to such pursuits. They are 'self-selected' in the sense that they are in some way predisposed – interested, stimulated, irritated, worried – to the undertaking. They are a special few. If among them the incidence of alienation is unusually high, it may be as much due to their intellectual temperament and curiosity as to their attainment in literacy.

The point of these comparisons is to suggest that, as with other aspects of civilisation, literacy or its absence is not a critical factor in the sort of alienation being considered. Factors such as status, self-image, confidence in one's culture and outlook are much more likely to explain why some people are more disturbed than others by encounters with or studies of other cultures.

My drift has plainly been to discount the costs of literacy in favour of its conveniences and advantages. Literacy has been a technology of incalculable use to human civilisation. Without it and its ancillary technologies indeed, much moral thought, current science, technology and literature simply could not exist. Even so, given our future-oriented outlook, we can ask whether literacy is an aid which may soon be dispensable. Has it – to wax poetic – helped sow the seeds of its own redundancy? Are transistors and micro-electronics moving in to displace it? The technology for storing information, for instance, has so advanced that the *Encyclopaedia Britannica* can be stored in a computer and have its facts, interpretations and illustrations updated annually. Its next edition may emerge not in book form, but in some package of microfilm, even easier to store and consult than books. Journalists need no longer write their reports and articles, for a computer can take dictation from them. Their readers are already partially weaned on to radio and television while sound and video-recorders can store bulletins and features which are broadcast at times inconvenient to particular persons. Doubtless, it could be possible for authors and their readers to produce and to consume novels, treatises and histories in analogous fashion. Could the human race look forward then to discarding the alphabet and replacing it with some technology more efficient, perhaps much more powerful in aiding the human mind to understand and wisely use itself and the worlds about it? If we can, we shall have another instance of the observation that things come to their fullest flowering at the very point of incipient obsolescence: literacy will face discard, on the very verge of being disseminated universally.

Before we explore this question, let us pause for three brief remarks. First, we recall that literacy is a visual vehicle of language and thought: it is both a substitute and a supplement for communication by speech. What we are considering then really comprises three questions: is there a possibility of a visual medium of language more efficient than the ninety or so existing alphabets; more radically, is there a possibility of dispensing with a visual medium altogether; and, more moderately, might more faculties be harnessed to enhance thought and communication?

Second, we are not talking about the immediate future. If anything, we are speculating about the middle twenty-first century. For, even if the means to enable the lapse of literacy are already available, the very mass of extant written material, the habits of the current generation of humanity and the interests vested in promoting and profiting from literacy would ensure a momentum to keep it in use for several decades yet.

Third, in our considerations we shall again require to bear simultaneously in mind several kinds of writers and readers. At one extreme are people who might read only local advertisements and bed-time stories to their children – a humble enough function, but, in the view of some psychologists, of much importance in the sound development of children. These same persons may use writing only to send greetings cards on festal occasions and to sign such documents as forms for family allowances and the school reports of their children. At the other extreme are people whose livelihood is derived from reading and writing – journalists, secretaries, typists. In between are a range of people to whom literacy, although not in constant use, is either essential or highly convenient. From a slightly different angle, we can think of those who use literacy as a routine and humdrum technology and equally of those few who use it carefully, painfully even, to refine their thoughts and to advance the frontiers of human understanding. My intent in stressing this is to try to avoid allowing the discussion to be unwittingly biased by the requirements of only a restricted portion of the users of literacy.

That there is a need to devise either an alternative or an extension to literacy was intimated in the discussion of the technologies ancillary to it. We noted that in the processes of formulating and receiving messages technology had not made strides comparable to those in storage, retrieval and dissemination. The capacities of the individual writer and reader can certainly be enhanced, but not to the spectacular pitch, say, of a web offset lithographic press. Yet it can be argued that large numbers of routine but intensive users of literacy need to have their formulating, and still more their receiving, capacities stepped up well beyond present limits. Striking examples are heads of state, their auxiliary ministers and humbler aides. The streams of papers, memoranda, statistics they need to ingest and interpret are formidable. Less publicly, but quite as intensely, the officials of the international organisations of the United Nations, the European Economic Community, the Organisation of Petroleum Exporting Countries, and the multitude of transnational corporations are receiving, sifting, interpreting, condensing, disseminating almost incessant flows of information and advice. In the professions, research, experiment, development and publication proceed at such a pace and diversity that their members are compelled to devise strategies of selection and sampling to ensure that they can keep abreast without dissipating their energies or drowning in the mass of reading matter.

While these people may indeed form relatively small minorities of their countries – even tinier ones of the world's population at large – they also constitute a very critical minority. In their hands lies the formation not simply of the day-to day decisions on economic and social policy, but equally significantly of the foundations for the future. The efficiency with which they can grapple with information and synthesise several strands into judgments and decisions is of obvious importance to the human race as a whole.

To those who hold democratic values, it is also important that the majorities of people should have an adequate understanding of what the minorities are up to and be able to exercise some intelligent and informed control over them. Already it is arguable that even very literate citizens in relatively democratic polities find themselves unable to maintain a satisfactory grasp of the workings of their societies. The very complexity of social organisation and interaction generates massive flows of information from several sources, often competing and inconsistent with each other. Pooling the mass and balancing off the biases are tricky processes. Many of their less literate compatriots indeed regard the effort as hopeless. They either withdraw themselves from it or surrender themselves to dogged prejudice. (In polities which put more trust in oligarchy and authoritarianism – benevolent, repressive, or both at once – the burden on the ordinary citizens is lighter, if only because less information is vouchsafed to them.)

The central problem is, of course, not literacy but the volume of information which needs to be communicated, received, processed. At present, however, literacy is the major technology available for enabling people to handle it and is increasingly unequal to the task, the growth of which it has itself facilitated.

Hence we have our three questions. It will be convenient to recall them in slightly more elaborate form. Are there possibilities of a visual and precise medium of the spoken word, which can replace the alphabet? Can there be a total replacement of such a medium, so that the eye need no longer assist the receipt, retention or the formulation of complex sets of words? Can further faculties be mobilised to reinforce those already co-ordinated in the application of literacy?

One way to approach these queries would be to proceed much as we did with the ancillary technologies. Only, instead of reviewing processes, we can look at the actual detailed uses of literacy and assess whether some other technology might fill them more effectively.

A very rudimentary, but highly important, application of writing is signing one's own name – bank cheque, legal documents, tax returns are among the forms which currently require signatures. However, for centuries and even now where literacy is not universal, people have managed by merely making their mark. While such an expedient certainly has its uses, it also has obvious drawbacks and, for any important occasion, has had to be confirmed by a witness. The signature was an advance on the mark. There are now at least four further advances which could render the signature obsolete. All four offer greater reliability and surer protection from cheats, but not yet complete invulnerability. The memorised password or number – for collecting money from machines, instead of bank tellers, for instance – the finger-print, the photograph and the voice-print may soon make it unnecessary to learn how to write one's own name, much less develop a distinctive signature. The alphabet and visual word would become redundant. The eye, on the other hand, although released from association with sound and meeting, would be required nevertheless to maintain a keen capacity for discrimination.

Storage and retrieval were the uses to which the merchants and bankers of Sumer and Babylon put their scratchings on tablets. They remain major day-to-day uses for government offices, judiciaries, commercial and industrial enterprises of all kinds and magnitudes. They are important also to less mighty people, like the housewife who jots down a shopping list or reminder, the officials who note appointments and family birthdays in diaries, the doctor who makes a list of house calls, the secretary of a voluntary society who has to produce minutes – but not verbatim records – of discussions and decisions, the school-child who notes what has to be done for homework. In vaster volume, books, textbooks and libraries exist precisely to store matters for others to retrieve conveniently. But retrieval is not always a matter of just dipping into a number of references and memorising them. It often also demands noting down particularly salient facts and comments, so that reading carefully can entail selective copying-by-writing. Where people own their own books – and even where they do not – important passages may provoke underlinings, queries, expostulations in the margins.

Clay tablets were in time replaced by paper files and red tape. These in their turn are beginning to be displaced by microfilm and computer tape. Although these developments may signal the end of the file, the book or even the page, as we know them, they do not necessarily entail the end of visual words. At the moment, indeed, they store and reproduce their information almost entirely in the form of written words. However, it is possible to conjecture that the storage could be arranged in the form of sound, so that 'looking up' a book or memorandum would mean having it read out by machine. Such a change – a shift of emphasis back to aural communication – would be acceptable at large only under a good number of conditions.

First, the average person's span of aural retention would need to be increased. It is well attested, for instance, that at the end of a forty minute lecture most listeners who do not take notes are hard put to it to recall more than the most striking points uttered. As these observations have been made in literate societies, generally among more than usually literate people, like university students, it can be hypothesised at least that a decrease of dependence on literacy may yield a corresponding increase in aural abilities. Enhancing the span of aural attention may then prove no difficulty.

Second, it should be possible to scan or sample a memo or book easily, so as to identify rapidly whether it is relevant and which parts of it seem to be most relevant to whatever purpose is in hand.

Third, the time taken to consult what has to be consulted should be no longer than would be needed by reading. At present, people can readily learn how to read silently in English at the rate of 500 and more words per minute. This is about double the rate of a person reading aloud or even speaking rapidly. Even if machines could produce 500 spoken words clearly per minute, the listener would have to be sure he could understand and retain what was being said without having frequently to resort to replays.

Fourth, it must be possible to refer back and to check earlier statements with no more inconvenience than is currently entailed with written material.

Fifth, it must be possible easily to abstract notes, summaries and quotes.

Sixth, where statistical material is involved, there will need to be a way of presenting its tables, so that they can support or be supported by the text. A similar condition would of course apply to diagrams and other illustrations.

Seventh, the system must be at least as reliable and insensitive to minor careless use as written material is.

Eighth, of course, its equipment would need to be as portable and as accessible as books.

Ninth, it must be possible to do all this privately in public rooms and places without disturbing the larger public.

Finally, of course, such an aural system must cost no more than acquiring, keeping and consulting books and their ilk.

Taken together, these ten conditions suggest that it is unlikely that solely sonic or aural forms of storage and retrieval would easily satisfy what literacy satisfies at present.

If that line of exploration seems provisionally fruitless, there is at least the conceptual possibility of using electric impulses without any intervening medium at all. At present the impulses stored in a computer have to be converted into visual – pictorial, alphabetic or numerical – or sonic symbols in order to concord with the normal human modes of perception. Might it be possible for such impulses to be conducted directly to a person's brain without the medium of either sound or vision? Such a question would draw us into the area of some form of radio communication or mental telepathy, a realm so ill understood that we shall not attempt to enter it. Suffice it to suggest that only through some such quantum leap in the ability of the human mind to deal with large volumes of information will literacy become redundant for storage and retrieval.

Even if large-scale, formally disseminated modes of storage will probably not dispense with literacy, can the same be said of the smaller, more particular and personal conveniences, like the minutes of club committees, shopping lists and so on? The answer is more likely negative, for at this very moment people could use tape-recorders and pocket-dictating-machines for such purposes, and perhaps some do. The main barrier to their wider use at present is their cost and fragility, compared with the cheapness and availability of scraps of paper and pencils. If the examples of computers, pocket-calculators and electric typewriters can be bases for

prediction, considerable falls in costs coupled with improvements in convenience, toughness and variety of usages
can be expected for the analogues of today's dictaphones.
Diaries and future appointments present a problem which is
different, but in principle no less soluble. If even clockwork
alarms can be set for twelve hours ahead, electronic calendars
should be able to cope with twelve months. 'Appointments
Secretaries', dealing with birthdays, anniversaries and other
festivals, should be within easy grasp of electronics and sonics
to handle without recourse to visuals at all.

Similarly in casual personal correspondence – where it
survives the telephone and successors – the obsolescence of
the paper-borne letter and greetings card can easily be
foreseen. The spoken word in one form or another will be
easier to despatch. New means of transmission may make
even a written address unnecessary. But what about
'emergency' messages popped through letter boxes, pinned on
doors, left on desks, clutched importantly by children?
'Dropped by for a word – will be back round ten', or 'Join us
at the pub to celebrate Carol's engagement', or 'Could you
lend us a pint of milk for breakfast, please?' These rare little
contingencies cannot by any means be termed central to life.
Neither can the convenience of meeting them with literacy be
gainsaid. Replacing paper and pencil here easily and cheaply
seems likely to present difficulty. It may even fail to present a
sufficient challenge to the technological innovators.

Advertising is an activity which mobilises all the media to
appeal to the full range of human sensibility – aural, visual,
tactile, olfactory, sexual, competitive. Currently, it appeals
most to the visual sense, simply because the visual channels
are the most easily exploited – television screens, roadside
posters, magazines, newspapers. A natural consequence is
that the written word remains important. Indeed, it mostly
carries the critical elements of an advertising message. Note
for instance how on the television or cinema screen the
written word is used to drive home the impressions blazed by
the pictorial and spoken persuasions. If economics continue
to permit and encourage the production of many versions of

one commodity – seven brands of petrol, for example, in Britain, as against only one in Mexico and a number of other states – and if competitive advertising continues to be permitted, it would be silly to suppose that advertisers would stop using visual media to promote sales. Could they, however, stop using the written word, if the rest of society had been able much to reduce its use of it? Probably not, because the need for distinguishing marks of name and of quality would drive the advertisers willy-nilly to invent new visual codes of their own.

To be sure, firms and other institutions already have their own logograms and ways have been devised of signalling with two or three signs rather than a dozen words how certain goods and fabrics should or should not be treated. The eloquence of these is, however, extremely limited and could scarcely convey to the public the profusion of virtues which the advertisers burst to tell. How could a picture or two put their fingers on the 'fingerlickinhighkickintastegrabbinmind-smashinnukefizzindollywowin . . .' etc. delights wrapped in a single mouthful of a certain refreshment? Language itself, even when supported by the latest gimmicks of cinematography, is strained to meet the urgencies of the advertisers. Unless language itself is replaced and ways are invented of getting pictures to signal precise and unambiguous verbal messages without the aid of written words, the advertisers are not likely to forgo the uses of literacy.

If this supposition is true of advertisers prominent in the public eye, it is probably even truer for the humbler forms of advertising. Small cards on notice-boards in shops and estate agents' windows, the columns of classified advertisements in local newspapers, the fly-sheets for local meetings, jumble sales, fetes and concerts, the notices of plans for buildings and highways, the descriptive labels and pricetags on goods for sale are all minor specimens of communication by literacy. They are the uses which lubricate the flow and exchange of humdrum but valuable information almost without being noticed. Illiterate societies and illiterate people in literate societies have indeed managed without them, for they are not essential. They could disappear without much damage to society. Yet since such advertising does serve purposes for numbers of people of all strata of society, it is likely to evaporate only if something equally cheap, convenient and effective comes into being.

One such possible replacement, again brought within reach by the computer, parallels current services on the telephone. People can already obtain recipes, weather forecasts, news of important sports events, the sounds of the latest musical hit, even bed-time stories. No great effort is needed then to think of an advertising service, like a dynamic talking *Yellow Pages* up-dated from minute to minute. It could be asked for lists of second-hand models of certain makes of cars of certain vintages and specifications, what vacancies might be available for part-time charity pool collectors or space-walkers, who might be looking for an old piano or laser can-opener; who might be offering rejuvenating massages or lessons in mental karate. On the other hand, such lists might well entail the enquirer's having to store the information for later use. He could jot it down, using literacy. Or it could be recorded for later visual display, using reading only. Or the lists could be recorded by sound only and moved through with no use of literacy at all.

To puncture this vision, so easily dreamed in a relatively affluent society, let us remind ourselves for a moment that it might need a century or more, before the poorer communities of the world could take up such a service. They would need to depend for a while on common or garden literacy. Might literacy, once the preserve of the rich and powerful, be cast off for the poor and primitive to use in their minor domestic bartering?

For most of this book, I have discussed literacy as a technology of usefulness – in accounts, administration, communication, scientific thought. The service it gives to the lighter sides of human life has scarcely been touched. Yet entertainment – serious, comic, violent, horrific, puzzling, challenging (think of crosswords or the game of Scrabble) – accounts for a sizeable proportion of the reading matter published. The figures given in an earlier chapter suggest that the appetite for entertainment has not been sated by television, radio, theatre or cinema. Indeed, it is precisely in the countries richest in these media that the use of public libraries and the growth of printed materials have been greatest.

This coincidence of facts is partly explained by the prior coincidence of widely distributed wealth, leisure and literacy. Another part of the explanation lies in the nature of entertainment by literacy and its advantages over other forms. Consider the illustration of the modern traveller. He is not an insignificant person: in Britain more than 700 million passenger journeys are made by rail annually and more than 30 million people use the airports. Proportionately similar statistics will apply to other countries in the same category of industrialisation and wealth. At all major railway stations and airports and on passenger ships of any size, travellers will find sizeable bookstalls in states of evident busyness and prosperity. The meaning of this phenomenon is obviously that travellers do a lot of reading. Their circumstances explain why. In the first place, they will have to pass some time sitting – if they are fortunate, even standing – in a restricted space, in somewhat crowded conditions, in the company of strangers with whom conversation may prove desultory and fitful, if it occurs at all. Unless they are skilled at meditation, engrossed in the land, sea or airscape or content to be still, they will seek some activity which satisfies them without at all inconveniencing their fellow-travellers or attracting opprobrium. Reading is clearly one such. Because books, magazines and most newspapers are compact, it trespasses on no further space. Because only the reader reads, neither additional human help nor auxiliary machinery are required. Because for most people nowadays reading is a silent activity, it disturbs no neighbour – unless the matter proves uproariously comic. Reading is also an activity which the reader tailors to his own convenience and which does not require the reader to adapt his schedule to another timetable, as radio, cinema, theatre and television ordinarily do. That is, it can be fitted in with whatever time happens to be available. An extension of this aspect is that reading can be taken up, stopped and recommenced at will. Since travel is studded with distractions and interruptions of various sorts, this is a not inconsiderable advantage, as is the possibility of referring back easily and quickly to pick up lost threads.

Equally important, the traveller can choose what he wants to read and make his selection from a much more extensive range of choice than other forms of entertainment afford. To these advantages are added three more. One is the factor of cost: most books for entertainment can be bought in formats which permit the expense to be regarded as a minor consumption, rather than a major investment. The second is portability, for most reading material can be easily stowed away and carried. The third is permanence, for the reader does not have to pay again to re-read his book, nor need he wait for some company to do a repeat performance. As Thucydides wanted his history to be, a book or a magazine can, if the traveller so decides, be a 'possession for ever'.

These observations, although made of people who have few alternatives to reading, catalogue a formidable battery of advantages. Can they be rivalled? The recent improvements to hearing aids, the development of pocket video-screens and the promise of the silicon chip in storing, retrieving and manipulating astonishing quantities and types of information forbid a firmly negative response. On the contrary, they conjure the possibility of having the entire, unabbreviated works of, say, Dickens, Tolstoy or Shakespeare contained in the space of a thumb-nail. Retrieval might be entirely sonic or a combination of visual and sonic narrative and drama. Some easy mechanism for 'flipping back' or finding a lost place or a quotation should not prove beyond human ingenuity. Station and airport bookstalls may eventually supplement, if not replace, their stocks of books with 'chips' of novels and collections of short stories. The more intense compactness of the 'chip' may in fact enable the stalls to offer their customers even wider and cheaper choices than now.

If such a rivalling of literacy were successful in satisfying the needs of travellers, there is little doubt that it would satisfy the mass of less constrained readers also. Actually reading for pleasure might become the preserve of those who write for pleasure and of conservationists reluctant to let go of an ancient and once important human skill.

Nevertheless, although the need for literacy may well shrink, it may at the same time become further entrenched. For how might the narrations and dramatisations be achieved, unless the writers, editors, revisionists, adaptors, narrators and actors could study and learn the texts in detail? An implication here is that, for the masses to enjoy literature without literacy, a minority would need to be highly literate. The paradox evokes two reflections on technological change. One is that, as science and technology introduce new changes in production and services, a growing majority with decreasing skills seems to become increasingly dependent on a highly skilled but shrinking minority. The trend appears to lead to a dictatorship of technocrats. On the other hand, while a necessary consequence of the extension of specialisation may well be the dependence of majorities upon minorities, oppressive technocracy is not the necessary end. The reason is simply that the proliferation of specialisations generates a net of interdependence and a homeostatic distribution of power.

The second reflection is to hark back to the discussion on the social repercussions of changes in production and consumption. A general drift from reading would transform, perhaps almost annihilate, the paper and printing industries. Counterbalancing this would be the multiplying demand for good writers, narrators, actors, camera and sound effects people, cameras, microphones and all the paraphernalia and ancillaries which go with them. There would ensue the usual mixture of dislocation, adjustment, disruption and loss for some, new opportunities for others.

The most important use of literacy, perhaps the most unexpected to those who invented it, and, as we have seen, often the most neglected, is its function as a technology of the intellect. Literacy, we have suggested, has been the major enabling technology in the development of reason, logic, systematic thinking and research. A brief recapitulation of how this comes about may be helpful:

1 Because the words are fixed before author or student, they become concretely manipulable, and elements against which the mind can react. They acquire these qualities, whether they are written in complete linear phrases and sentences or simply as mnemonics or in diagrammatic forms.

2 In these forms they enable re-reading, checking for logic, internal consistency, ellipses, redundancies, the smooth development and sequencing of thought, legitimate deductions and hypotheses, adequate accounting for facts. They obviate forgetting parts of arguments.

3 The reaction or response is, where dissatisfaction is felt, to revise, rephrase, refine, re-order, attempt new sequences or development, incorporate additional information or speculation, demolish and begin over again.

4 The processes of reaction may release fresh associations between submerged insights, spark slightly or radically new interpretations, stimulate further processes of enquiry, promote serendipities.

5 Written texts enable virtually simultaneous comparisons between accounts, versions and interpretations of the same phenomena and events. Comparisons reveal points common and divergent, and hence stimulate attempts at reconciliation.

I find it difficult to conceive how all these processes might be satisfactorily managed without the aid of some system of stable and manipulable visual symbols of language and thought. To say this is not to argue that paper and pencil or typewriter will continue to be necessary. The video-screen capable of displaying several images separately and simultaneously – and storing them safely – is already with us, and so is the electronic pencil-and-eraser. That is, the technologies ancillary to formulation and revision may change. Neither is it to argue that written words and sentences as we know them will always be indispensable: mathematics and symbolic logic, to name only two disciplines, make us wiser. That is, the alphabet may cease to be the most useful medium of literacy. My speculation is simply that human intellectual advance will continue to depend indefinitely upon some form of literacy.

The drift of the examination so far has been that literacy may become irrelevant to large areas of everyday communication, commerce, politics, administration, domestic life and leisure, but that it will probably remain necessary to the development of human thought, scholarship, science and technology and to the provision of literature for leisure. If we suppose that this prognosis has some plausibility, what might it signify for the universal right to literacy and for compulsorily teaching all children the three Rs?

If the areas of frequent and necessary application of literacy shrank considerably, the skills could cease to be needed for access to information, for safeguarding rights, for informed participation in social life and culture or for earning a decent living. The basis for declaring it a human right would fall away. Simultaneously, the very fact that it was no longer a widely useful skill would cause large numbers of those who had learned it, like the young Burmese noblemen, to let it lapse into disuse. Literacy might well become the art of a devoted minority.

In such case, the issue would be debated whether reading and writing should be taught at schools from the very earliest years as the very core of the curriculum, as is the case at present, or whether it should be treated as an option, to be taken up by people, as and when they find it appropriate. On the one hand, it is known that the ability of children to learn reading and writing is conditioned by their maturation, that at least four years of good tuition and practice are generally required to assure at least permanent literacy and that adults attain proficiency much more rapidly than children. These grounds might counsel dropping literacy from the curriculum of the primary school. It might be more efficient to introduce it to fourteen- and fifteen-year-olds who showed some likelihood of joining the 'devoted minority' and to keep open the option for later acquisition to those who later in life developed an interest which needed literacy. The under-fourteens could be turned to other learning, to social and 'survival' skills.

On the other hand, there might be hesitations about losing the possible desirable side-effects of an early training in literacy. There is no doubt that learning to read and write does help discipline the memory, promotes fine co-ordination between language, eye and fingers, and demands the methodical application of principles and rules. It might thereby help lay the foundations of good learning in the variety of other subjects and skills pursued in schooling. The loss of its contribution might create unforeseen difficulties to learning in other areas.

Voicing such uncertainties could be dismissed as the sort of superstitious conservatism that has kept Latin so long as a criterion for entering certain universities. An argument can be made that any form of structured, systematic and guided learning will have the same effects as training in literacy. Yet combining so many faculties as need to be marshalled to get something written, may have psychological benefits which cannot be replicated by simpler forms of learning. The debate cannot of course be settled here: as we have repeated often, the state of knowledge and research on the ramifications of the exercise of literacy is still far from complete.

Nevertheless, speculation like this suggests questions which, if researched and elucidated now, might illuminate decisions which may one day need to be taken. Literacy remains essential to the conduct of and participation in the life of today's industrialising, urbanising, modernising, nation-states. It remains the almost unquestioned basis of almost any activity dignified by the label 'education'. But since large pools of illiteracy persist alongside, opportunities exist patiently to explore the effects of literacy on the process of human learning and reasoning and to determine whether or not they might be dispensable in a society, which put little reliance on visual recording and communication.

If literacy were indeed to prove dispensable, an interesting reversal would occur. Once, the skills of reading and writing were the prerogative of the few. These privileged ones had knowledge, authority, power, access even to the godhead and the riddles of the universe. Literacy was denied to the masses, indeed held in awe by them. The redundancy of literacy would make it again the province of the few. But these few would busy themselves with something which the masses had actually cast off.

Further reading

Kathleen Gough (1968), 'Implications Of Literacy in Traditional China and India', in Jack Goody (1968), *Literacy In Traditional Societies*, London, Cambridge University Press, pp. 70–84.

Bibliography

Bibliography

Note
This list of references is by no means a full, let alone complete, bibliography of works on literacy. For something of that nature, David Harman's book is a good point of departure. Alternatively, the International Institute for Adult Literacy Methods, P.O. Box 1555, Tehran, Iran, has published a number of bibliographies.
Works marked * are suggested for further reading.

* Anderson, C. Arnold and Bowman, Mary Jean, eds (1966), *Education And Economic Development*, London, Frank Cass. Very useful collection of papers on the relationships between literacy, schooling and economic development.
* Bataille, Leon, ed. (1976), *A Turning Point For Literacy*, London, Pergamon Press. Useful for a survey of the state of illiteracy in the world in 1970 and for three case studies of national literacy programmes, Algeria, Peru and Viet Nam.
* Bowman, Mary Jean and Anderson, C. Arnold (1963), 'Concerning The Role Of Education In Development', pp. 247–79 in Clifford Geertz (1963), *Old Societies And New States*, New York, Free Press. A study of the statistical correlations between education and various indices of economic development.
* Cipolla, Carlo (1969), *Literacy And Development In The West*, Harmondsworth, Pelican. Traces the growth of Literacy in Europe in an interesting and entertaining style.
  Clammer, John (1976), *Literacy And Social Change: A Case Study of Fiji*, Leiden, E. J. Brill.
* Diringer, David (1968) (3rd edn), *The Alphabet – A Key To The History Of Mankind*, London, Hutchinson, 2 vols. A comprehensive history of writing, with a whole volume of illustrations.
* Downing, John, ed. (1975), *Comparative Reading: Cross-National Studies Of Behaviour And Processes In Reading and Writing*, New York, Macmillan. The title is self-explanatory.
* Freire, Paolo (1970), *Pedagogy Of The Oppressed*, New York,

Herder & Herder. One of the very influential books on the philosophy and politics of literacy and learning.

Gadgil, D. R. (1955), 'Report of Investigation into the Problems of Lapse into Illiteracy in Satara District', in D. R. Gadgil and V. M. Dandekar, *Primary Education in Satara District*, Publication no. 32, Pune (India), Gokhale Institute of Economics and Politics.

* Gelb, I. J. (1963) (2nd edn), *A Study of Writing*, University of Chicago Press. A history of writing, more compact than Diringer's, with some provocative theses.

* Goody, Jack, ed. (1968), *Literacy In Traditional Societies*, London, Cambridge University Press. Very useful collection of essays and studies on the uses made of literacy in a variety of societies.

Gray, William (1956), *The Teaching Of Reading And Writing*, Paris, UNESCO.

* Guthrie, John T., ed. (1976), *Aspects of Reading Acquisition*, Baltimore, Johns Hopkins University Press. Interesting collection of papers on the neurology and psychology of reading.

* Harman, David (1974), *Community Fundamental Education*, Lexington, D. C. Heath. Useful survey of attempts to define literacy and of efforts to promote literacy among adult illiterates. Very practical proposals for planning literacy programmes.

Hoyles, Martin, ed. (1977), *The Politics Of Literacy*, London, Writers and Readers Publishing Cooperative. Collection of papers and items on the social or class dimensions of literacy.

*Inkeles, Alex and Smith, David H. (1974), *Becoming Modern*, London, Heinemann. A study of the relationship between literacy and 'the modernisation syndrome' among several hundred people in a number of developing countries.

Inkeles, Alex and Holsinger, D., eds (1974), *Education And Individual Modernity In Developing Countries*. Provides more examples and discussions on the theme of the previous reference.

IEA. - International Association For The Evaluation of Educational Achievement (1973), *Reading Comprehension Education In Fifteen Countries*, by Robert L. Thorndike, New York, Wiley.

Iraq, Government of (1974), Act No. 142, Baghdad, Ministry of Information.

Lerner, Daniel (1958), *The Passing Of Traditional Society*, New York, Free Press. A fascinating study of the correlates of modernisation.

McLuhan, Marshall (1962), *The Gutenberg Galaxy*, London, Routledge & Kegan Paul. Provocative, if dogmatic and unsubstantiated, exploration of the effects of the printed word.

* Rogers, Everett M. and Shoemaker, F. (1971), *Communication Of Innovations: A Cross-cultural Approach*, New York, Free Press. An examination of the role of literacy and schooling in facilitating the spread and adoption of innovations, mainly in agricultural practices.

* Versluys, J. D. N. (1977), 'What Does A Literacy Course Achieve?', pp. 569–99 in *Teaching Reading And Writing To Adults: A Sourcebook*, Tehran, International Institute For Adult Literacy Methods. Useful survey of studies on the social and psychological effects of learning to read and write.